BRAIN RESEARCH
AND
CHILDHOOD EDUCATION

——•——

Implications for
Educators

Doris Bergen
and
Juliet Coscia

Association for Childhood Education International
17904 Georgia Avenue, Suite 215, Olney, Maryland 20832 • 800-423-3563 • www.acei.org

Anne W. Bauer, ACEI Editor
Bruce Herzig, ACEI Editor

Library of Congress Cataloging-in-Publication Data
Bergen, Doris.
    Brain research and childhood education: implications for educators/Doris Bergen
and Juliet Coscia.
      p. cm.
    Includes bibliographic references.
    ISBN 0-87173-154-1 (pbk.)
    1. Child development. 2. Education, Preschool. 3. Brain--Research. I. Coscia, Juliet.
II. Title.

LB1117.B4716 2001
612.8'2'02437--dc21

                                                    2001045698

TABLE OF CONTENTS

INTRODUCTION

In recent years, the educational media has given educators advice derived from various interpretations of brain research findings. The brain is now the "hot topic" for workshops and other inservice training. Although much of this advice and training is useful insofar as it provides educators knowledge about brain development, much is simplistic and misleading. This is especially true of advice concerning the implications of brain research for educational practice. Some writers (e.g., Bruer, 1999; Puckett, Marshall, & Davis, 1999) caution educators against over-interpretations of brain research findings, and strongly suggest resisting the "brain-based" curriculum bandwagon until additional research can clarify the educational implications. A growing body of research does exist about the potential effects of early environmental experiences on very young children's neural network development. However, even this topic is in the early stages of exploration; existing brain research findings have not yet been systematically linked to the body of psychological and educational research on cognitive, social-emotional, and physical development, which also has expanded greatly over the past 10-15 years.

The authors of this book believe educators could benefit from a publication that specifically addresses developmentally relevant brain research findings from a scientifically sound perspective and that reviews the sound (and unsound!) implications of such research for childhood education. The need for this book is threefold. First, many educators received their professional preparation before information derived from brain research was included as part of university curriculum, and thus they need basic information about the brain. Second, if educators are to use brain research findings thoughtfully and effectively, this information must be linked to the existing development and learning knowledge base derived from psychological and educational research. Third, by gaining knowledge about brain research, educators can examine how their present practices mesh with this research, and reflect on how their educational practice might be explained or enhanced by such knowledge.

CONTENTS OF THE BOOK

The purpose of this book is to answer some of the questions that educators have about brain research, and to help them sort out facts from unsubstantiated claims regarding its implications for education. It draws on recent research to offer information about brain growth and neurological development, from the prenatal period to middle childhood (within a context of lifelong brain development), and about the relationship between environment and brain development. It makes appropriate connections between specific aspects of brain development and general cognitive, social-emotional, and physical development, and it addresses the implications of these relationships for childhood education. It also points out overextended assumptions and spurious recommendations about the effects of specific educational practices on brain growth and neurological development.

The first chapter provides a brief overview of when, why, and how the brain was studied in earlier centuries, and explains the methodological advances that have promoted current brain research and led to recent findings. In chapter two, readers will find basic information about brain structures and functions, which educators need in order to understand and evaluate possible brain/learning relationships. The next three chapters focus on specific age ranges (prenatal to age 3, age 3 to age 8, age 8 to age 14), and catalog what is now known about the developing brain at each age level. These chapters also suggest ways that children's cognitive, social-emotional, and physical development may be related to changes in brain structure or function, including brain development issues relevant to children with disabilities. Additional information examines how children's environment and genetic make-up may foster or impede brain growth and neurological development. Implications of all this research for educational practice are noted. The final chapter discusses policy and practice issues that educators will need to address, given recent media emphasis on the importance of enhancing brain development and claims being made for adopting "brain-based" curricula.

CHAPTER 1
THE BRAIN AS A TOPIC OF RESEARCH THROUGHOUT HISTORY

The recent emphasis on brain research may lead one to assume that the study of the brain is a new phenomenon, and that questions about how brain structures and functions are related to behavior have been asked only recently. On the contrary, the structures and functions of the brain have interested physicians, philosophers, and researchers since the earliest times. Even primitive people knew that the brain was a vital organ. Archaeological findings show what appear to be deliberate drilling of holes in human skulls (perhaps to relieve pressure from brain injury). Study of the relationships between the brain and learning processes is more recent; some systematic study began in the 18th century. Earlier scholars did not consider the brain to be the body organ most responsible for thought and emotion.

It is important for educators to know the history of brain research for three major reasons. First, this knowledge provides the basic context from which educators can view recent research and compare it to earlier findings. Second, historical information makes it clear that questions being asked now are not so different from those asked in the past; technological advances simply make accurate answers more likely. Third, the historical perspective highlights the brain's complexity and, hence, the challenge faced by researchers who are attempting to gain an accurate understanding of brain functioning. This perspective serves as a reminder that present research findings are only beginning to scratch the surface of the brain's relationship to cognitive, emotional, social, and other learning processes. Therefore, educators must still proceed with caution when making educational practice recommendations based on present brain research.

EARLY STUDY OF THE BRAIN

Evidence exists that, as early as 1700 B.C., Egyptian doctors used surgical practices to treat brain injuries; their observations led them to conjecture about connections between the central nervous system, sensation, and locomotion. The Egyptians, however, did not value the brain as much as other vital organs of the body. In their mummification process, they usually drained out the brain matter while carefully preserving the heart, liver, and other organs (Finger, 1994). By 450 B.C., Greek physicians and philosophers discussed the brain's functions in sensation and thought. For example, Alemaeon of Croton practiced dissection as a science and described the optic nerve as the "path of light to the brain" (Gross, 1998). Much early speculation about the human brain was generalized from study of dead animals and humans. Thus, a number of assumptions drawn from these sources (e.g., that human brains had cavities similar to sheep brains) were incorrect.

In Greece, a great debate ensued among philosophers as to whether the heart or the brain was the center of thought and the location of the soul. Although Plato saw the brain as the site of sensation and thought, Aristotle believed the brain was merely a means of cooling the "humours" of the blood. Aristotle's view that the heart was the major center of rationality held sway for centuries. This "cardiocentric" view may have contributed to the long period during the middle ages when there was little study of the brain. Nevertheless, despite the pervasive Aristotelian view, some physicians did study the structures of the brain and made suppositions about their functions. For example, Hippocrates saw a connection between the brain and nervous system disorders. He drilled holes in his patients' skulls to "restore balance of the humours." The Roman physician Galen identified the autonomic and sympathetic nervous systems and believed that wounds of the brain affected the mind. When he studied the convolutions of the cerebral cortex in donkeys, however, he concluded that this part of the brain could not be related to higher mental functions. The lack of importance attributed to this part of the brain by early researchers is demonstrated by its name—cortex means "bark" or "rind."

During the period from 400 B.C. to 100 A.D. (Finger, 1994; Gross, 1998), scholars in China, India, and Syria demonstrated interest in the brain. For example, Huang Di Nei Jing's study of the brain led him to assert that the skull was composed of marrow, similar to the substance in other bones of the body; and the Chinese believed there was a connection between the eyes and the brain (i.e., the evil eye). The Indian physician Charaka considered the heart to be the source of power and energy, while Nemesius of Syria proposed that specific sensory and motor functions were located in the ventricles (cavities) of the brain. This incorrect view of the ventricles was generally accepted throughout the middle ages.

Beginnings of "Scientific" Study

After the hiatus in interest during the middle ages, the Renaissance opened another period of brain study (Finger, 1994; Gross, 1998). In the 1500s, the anatomist Vesalius concluded that Galen's earlier description of brain anatomy was erroneous, and so he suggested some revisions. Leonardo da Vinci's illustrations of animal brains and his wax casts of the brain ventricles offered some of the first precise anatomical information about brain structures. Although his information did not agree with earlier illustrations of the brain, he did not challenge the idea that the ventricles were the source of sensory and motor functions.

Using the newly invented microscope, Malpighi studied the microscopic anatomy of the cortex in the 1600s. He concluded that it was made up of little glands with attached ducts (Gross, 1998), and this view of the brain as a glandular organ was commonly accepted in the 17th and 18th centuries. Microscopic study also resulted in speculation about the functions of the gyri (the bulging folds of the cerebral cortex). Willis suggested that the gyri controlled memory and will (Gross, 1998). Although Descartes identified the pineal gland and hypothesized about its function, he still asserted that the brain and the mind were two different entities. By the 1700s, scholars accepted the idea that various areas of the brain were responsible for specific functions and identified some of these sites. For example, Legallois isolated the medulla as the respiratory center of the brain. In the 1800s, other scientists also supported cortical localization, isolating separate motor and sensory cortical areas (Swedenborg), identifying the cerebellum as the site of movement coordination (Flourens), attributing motor control of language to the frontal cortex (Broca), and locating interpretation of spoken language in the temporal cortex (Wernicke) (Finger, 1994). (See Figure 1.) Unfortunately, the momentum for specifying which sections of the brain were responsible for various functions was interrupted as brain study was sidetracked by Gall's promotion of phrenology. Phrenology connects skull shape and features to various personality characteristics. Gall outlined a variety of characteristics that he believed were directly related to certain sections of the skull. However, Flouren's suggestion that the brain acts as a whole to form intelligence led to attacks on Gall's approach; by the late 1800s, phrenology was generally discounted.

Figure 1
Model of the Brain

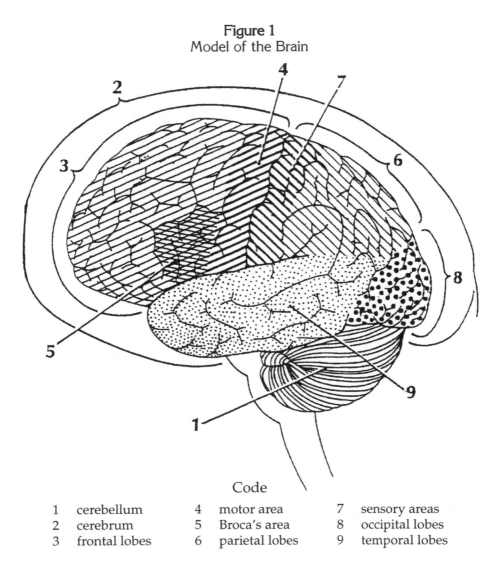

Code

1	cerebellum	4	motor area	7	sensory areas
2	cerebrum	5	Broca's area	8	occipital lobes
3	frontal lobes	6	parietal lobes	9	temporal lobes

Diagram from Brain Basics, *published by the National Institute of Neurological Disorders and Stroke.*

LATE 19TH AND EARLY 20TH CENTURY STUDY

Caton's "Neuron Doctrine," an important development in the late 1800s, stated that neurons were independent units composed of cell bodies, axons, and dendrites (Finger, 1994; Gross, 1998). The use of electrophysical recordings (another technological advance) to study electrical currents in the brain and improvements to the microscope enabled scientists to pinpoint more of the brain's functional/structural relationships. For example, Schwann identified the fat-like deposits on neuron axons (the myelin sheath), and Sherrington discovered the "spaces" between axon and dendrites (the synapses) and studied how messages were transmitted across those synapses.

By the early 1900s, there were several competing theories on how the brain functions. The strict localizationist theory emphasized brain areas as singly responsible for particular behaviors. At the other extreme was Lashley's (1950) equipotentiality theory, which in its strictest sense suggested that all areas of the brain contribute equally to all behaviors. Lashley later modified his theory to suggest that while specific regions of the brain are devoted to specific functions, each subarea of a given region is involved in that specific function to some extent. Luria (1973), a Russian neuropsychologist, developed yet another competing idea of the brain, one that described the brain as being composed of "functional systems." He believed that multiple areas of the brain function together to produce behavior, that functional systems are not unique, and that different systems may be responsible for any given behavior.

One of the first researchers who studied the brain's relation to learning was Franz (Finger, 1994), who studied the brain's ability to learn or relearn after it had been damaged. His findings suggested that new pathways could be developed after brain injury, thus supporting the more integrated theories of brain functioning.

By the early 20th century, most researchers agreed that the brain is composed of areas responsible for specific functions, but that as a whole it operates as a finely integrated unit. However, many mysteries remained as to how the structures of the brain actually function. In the mid to late 20th century, brain research made a major leap forward with the invention of sophisticated methods for studying animal brains and new technologies that could study the actions of the brain in living persons.

MID TO LATE 20TH CENTURY STUDY

Major technological advances have enabled brain researchers to engage in much more precise study. Metabolic, electrophysiologic, magnetic, and neuropsychological methods for studying living brains allow researchers to learn much more about the relationships between brain structures and functions. The information in this book is derived primarily from research using these procedures. Because the procedures are still being refined, implications for education based on findings from these procedures are hypotheses only. Figure 2 details the advantages and disadvantages of each procedure.

Metabolic Procedures

These procedures permit researchers to learn more about *where* thinking is occurring in the brain. They include positron emission tomography (PET), single photon emission tomography (SPECT), and functional magnetic resonance imaging (fMRI).

Figure 2
Advantages and Disadvantages of Current Brain Research Techniques

Technique	Advantages	Disadvantages
PET/SPECT	-Noninvasive -Able to localize brain activity -Able to use on young children	-Ethical questions about use of radioactive materials on children -Range of isolation of activity is centimeter range (imprecise) -Brief time span before decay of signal -Expensive
fMRI	-Noninvasive -No exposure to radiation -Precise, isolates areas in range of millimeters -Fast	-Participants must be very still -High level of noise may be painful -Cramped environment -Expensive
EEG	-Noninvasive -Sensitive to state changes -Relatively inexpensive	-Not really suited to study of cognitive processes -Poor spatial and temporal resolution
ERP	-Can examine cognitive activity -Each signal marked by specific event/stimulus so provides more accurate temporal information -More electrodes so provides more accurate spatial information -Many measures in brief time	-Errors occur if extraneous movement (muscles, eyes) occurs, resulting in loss of trial or cases
MSI/MEG	-Fast enough to track neural signals -Tracks neural pathways directly -Yields good spatial (in millimeters) and temporal (in milliseconds) data	-Only reads signals near brain surface -Extremely sensitive to outside magnetic fields (moving metal objects) -Expensive
Neuropsychological Assessment	-Noninvasive -Tasks can be used in animal research to make inferences about human behavior -Can be used with children and across lifespan	-Most tools measure more than one behavior, so difficult to isolate behaviors -Difficult to determine precise location of brain lesion or dysfunction

Developed from information in Nelson, C.A., & Bloom, F. E. (1997).
Child development and neuroscience. *Child Development, 68*(5), 970-987.

PET and SPECT. These procedures follow the flow and usage of radioactive compounds (e.g., oxygen or glucose for PET and technetium-99 or xenon-133 for SPECT) through the brain while the person is performing mental tasks. As the radioactive substance decays, a positron (positively charged electron-like particle) is emitted and tracked. High emissions from an area means high levels of oxygen or glucose are required in that area during cognitive activity; thus, the areas of greatest activity during particular tasks (e.g., naming pictures, reading, memorizing) can be observed. Chugani and colleagues (Chugani, Phelps, & Mazziotta, 1993) used this procedure to observe glucose use patterns and make inferences about the rapid development of synapses during infancy and childhood.

fMRI. Brain activity requires oxygen, which is carried by hemoglobin in blood cells. After losing oxygen to the cells, hemoglobin becomes magnetic (paramagnetism occurs) and thus can be tracked by fMRI. Areas of the brain that are working hard require more hemoglobin and thus generate more paramagnetic byproduct. Continuous scans at different orientations can provide cross-sectional images of the brain and allow researchers to compare brain activity during cognitive task vs. non-task periods. Kim, Ugurbil, and Strick (1994) used this procedure to discover that parts of the cerebellum play an important role in learning and problem solving. Using this same procedure, Cohen and Bookheimer (1994) found that the middle and inferior frontal gyri are active in children's nonspatial working memory.

Electrophysiologic Procedures

These procedures can be used to explore the question of *when* thinking is occurring. They include electroencephalogram (EEG) and event-related potentials (ERP).

EEG. In this procedure, electrodes fastened to the scalp monitor and record the electrical activity of the brain: a byproduct of neuronal communication. Using this procedure, Dawson and colleagues (Dawson, Klinger, Panagiotides, Hill, & Spieker, 1992) studied infants born to depressed mothers. They found that these infants showed greater activation of the right hemisphere as compared to infants of non-depressed mothers. Dawson and colleagues suggested that greater activation of the right hemisphere may indicate a greater vulnerability to internalizing disorders.

ERP. Using similar scalp-fastened electrode procedures, researchers using ERP flash stimuli in front of subjects and monitor resultant electrical activity in the brain. Benasich and Spitz (1998) used ERP to study children's language development and found that later language disorders could be predicted based on ERP findings in infancy.

Magnetic Procedures

To explore *where* and *when* thinking is occurring, magnetic source imaging (MSI) and magnetic encephalography (MEG) can be used. The very small magnetic field generated by each electrical neural signal can be monitored by superconducting quantum interference devices (SQUIDs), which track the neural signal along its pathway through the brain. Computer analysis of the signals then creates a visual map of this pathway. To date, the only studies of thinking using this method have focused on adult subjects.

Neuropsychological Assessment Procedures

These procedures rely on the assumption that brain function and behavior are causally related and that neuropsychological measurement techniques can be used to identify behavioral deficits related to brain functioning. Neuropsychological measures refer to tasks (some are paper-and-pencil, some are oral, some are presented via computer) that an examiner administers to patients in a one-on-one context. Researchers use neuropsychological measures to test hypotheses about specific brain functions, and assessment usually examines intellectual, memory, attention, language, sensory, motor, visuospatial, and executive functions. They also may focus on academic, social, and behavioral domains. Diamond and Goldman-Rakic (1989) examined the relationship between the prefrontal cortex and spatial working memory, using neuropsychological measures previously used with monkeys. Researchers have begun using these neuropsychological procedures in combination with fMRI or ERP techniques to enhance their understanding of the relationship between children's brain functioning and behavior.

SPECULATIVE COGNITIVE MODELS AND THEORIES OF BRAIN FUNCTIONING

In their discussion of the brain, Brash, Maranta, Murphy, and Walker (1990) suggest that "perhaps alone in all of nature, it is the only organ that is aware of itself, aware of the universe that surrounds it, aware of life and death" (p. 14). From the research base amassed over the past few decades, theorists have hypothesized other views of the overall function and structure of the brain, and even of its role in consciousness. For example, Crick (1994) speculates that scientists eventually will be able to explain the existence of consciousness by studying the brain's biological processes, and he is pursuing this question through a study of vision. Edelman (1992) challenges the prevailing view of the computer as the best metaphor for the brain (input, processing, output), suggesting instead that the brain can be considered an ecological system. He suggests that the brain is similar to the ecological system of a jungle, with its rich and complex dynamic interactions. The theories of scientists such as Crick and Edelman raise many new questions for research, and it is likely that brain research will continue for most of this century before these questions are answered. In their discussion of the brain, Ornstein and Thompson (1984) stated, "After thousands of scientists have studied it for centuries, the only word to describe it remains, amazing" (p. X). More recent findings continue to support that view.

IMPLICATIONS OF PAST RESEARCH FOR CHILDHOOD EDUCATION

Knowledge of when, why, and how the brain has been studied gives educators a perspective from which to view more recent research efforts. In particular, history shows that earlier ideas were not always correct, and that ongoing research using new technological advances may continue to change what appears to be "common knowledge" about the brain and learning. Thus, educators need to remain open-minded and committed to updating their own knowledge.

It is also important for educators to know about current research methods so that they can converse knowledgeably with neuropsychologists who may assess children they teach, and comprehend and interpret written information about findings of brain research that may affect educational practice. This review of past research points out that much more remains to be learned about the brain before educators can commit to using a particular "brain-based" curriculum. As more sophisticated research methods emerge, educators' knowledge about the brain's capacities for learning and the educational environments that best promote that learning will continue to change and grow.

THE BRAIN'S STRUCTURES AND FUNCTIONS

Most university programs that prepare educators have a minimal (or nonexistent) emphasis on relating learning theories and/or teaching strategies to brain development and functioning. When education students take biology, microbiology, or chemistry courses, they may consider these courses to be nothing more than liberal arts education requirements and not as sources of knowledge they will need as educators intending to facilitate children's learning. (The instructors of those courses may see no relationship either!) Although developmental and educational psychology courses usually include a brief overview of brain structures and functions, students generally find this information hard to assimilate and may believe the information to be unrelated to teaching. This reaction is partly the result of the as yet not fully determined relationships between brain structures and functions. It is also due to the "separatist" mindset of most students and faculty members. Recently, however, some curricular modules have integrated an understanding of brain development into early childhood education (Gilkerson, 2001).

Information about brain structures and functions can enlighten educators as to how brain growth and neurological development may contribute to learning. Without a firm basic knowledge of the structures and functions of the nervous system and the brain, however, educators cannot understand this research or critically evaluate its implications for educational practice. Therefore, this chapter is intended to change educators' mental schema regarding the brain from "terra incognita" to "terra cognita" (unknown to known land). Educators must develop their own meaningful mental schema of the brain if they are to assimilate current research findings on brain functioning. Scientists now have a relatively clear general picture of the basic components of the nervous system, the structures in the brain, and the role these components and structures play in human physical and mental functioning. Theorists also have proposed hypotheses about how the brain works, and have made models or metaphors of its structure and functions that can help educators (or anyone) construct their own mental schema to use in translating brain research into meaningful educational theory and practice.

ONE MODEL OF BRAIN STRUCTURE: THE TRIUNE BRAIN
One popular model of brain structure was proposed in 1978 by MacLean. He hypothesized that the human brain was "triune," with three structural levels that evolved separately over time. MacLean identified functions in each of these levels, which he labeled as "reptilian," "mammalian," and "neomammalian." (See Figure 3.) Recent research calls into question some of MacLean's assumptions, especially in regard to the midbrain level. Nevertheless, the model still has some usefulness as a functional metaphor (Cytowic, 1993). In MacLean's model, the brain stem, medulla, pons, and cerebel-

Figure 3
Model of Triune Brain

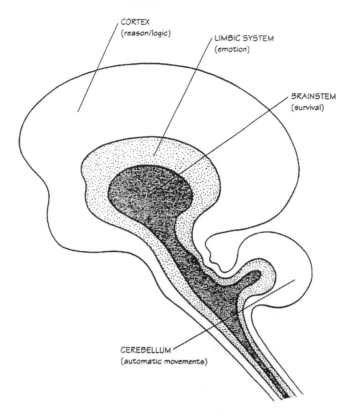

lum, which are responsible for basic body survival functions (such as breathing and balance), compose the "reptilian" brain (or the "hindbrain"). This was the earliest part of the brain to develop in humans. He identified the "mammalian brain" (or "midbrain") as part of the "limbic system," which includes the thalamus, hypothalamus, amygdala, corpus callosum, hippocampus, and pituitary gland, all of which have some responsibility for monitoring emotional and cognitive states. He hypothesized that the cerebrum ("neomammalian" or "forebrain") developed most recently because it is primarily responsible for complex thought. Other researchers posit that the brain is less hierarchical than in MacLean's system, and that the limbic system has greater importance in higher thought processes than he suggested (Sylwester, 1995). His model does provide a way for non-scientists (e.g., educators) to organize information about the brain's structures and develop a general mental schema. To really understand the brain, however, it is necessary to build upon such simple models, taking into consideration the circular functions essential for brain functioning, the neuronal networks, and the specific structural areas of the brain that control various functions.

The Neuronal Network

The neurons carry out the communication functions of the brain; each neuron is composed of a cell body, one axon (sending unit), and a number of dendrites (receiving units). Gaps between the axon and dendrites of each neuron are called synapses. Each neuron communicates through electrical impulses, which are sent through the axon and dendrites and, using chemical agents (neurotransmitters), "jump the gap" at the synaptic site. Over 100 neurotransmitters are activated by the correct "fit" with certain receptor sites. Each class of neurotransmitters appears to be involved with particular categories of activation, such as memory or emotional arousal (Lezak, 1995). The brain also contains blood vessels that nourish the neurons, thus enabling them to function. Brain tissues are extremely oxygen-dependent, and therefore rely greatly on the oxygen transmitted through these blood vessels (Powers, 1990). Although the brain weighs only about 3 pounds in adults (about 2 percent of an adult's total weight), it uses about 25 percent of the adult's blood supply. Figure 4 illustrates the basic neuronal communication system.

At birth, infant brains contain about 100 billion neurons, each of which can produce up to 15,000 synapses when they are well-nourished and adequately stimulated (Lezak, 1995). From birth to age 3, synapses increase greatly and continue to increase during the early childhood years. "This elaboration of neurons and increased synaptic potential constitutes the neural basis of learning, knowledge, ability, and skill" (Lezak, 1995, p. 47). These alterations in the brain's circuitry add to the brain's "long-term potentiation" for flexible and varied human behavior. Although some pruning occurs at earlier ages (Lichtman, 2001), that process takes off by age 8 or 9; synapses that have not been activated frequently start to disappear. Evidence suggests that dendritic growth can continue at later age levels, when new information is learned and used (Thompson & Nelson, 2001). It is believed that neurons in the central nervous system do not replenish themselves if they are injured, however, thus disrupting the circuits to which they contribute. Other cells may take over the disrupted function; if too many neurons are injured, however, that circuit usually cannot be reactivated.

The messages sent by neurons in the brain travel among the structures of the brain and also through the spinal cord to the nerves in the rest of the body. The brain and spinal cord together form the central nervous system (CNS). Supporting glia cells provide a fatty substance (myelin) that coats the axons, making message transmission faster and more efficient. Recent research indicates that one type of glia (astrocytes) may serve a number of other functions, such as supplying neurons with glucose, blocking toxic substances, and stimulating the generation of synapses (Netting, 2001). They also may store memory information and strengthen neural messages between neurons (Netting, 2001). Within the brain, neurons from various structures communicate with one another; those concerned with processing emotions are in communication with those involved in rational decision-making, and both communicate with the autonomic system. If a child is fearful, therefore, this emotion may interfere with the child's ability to learn and remember information, and it also may cause physical stress symptoms, such

Figure 4
Neuronal Communication System

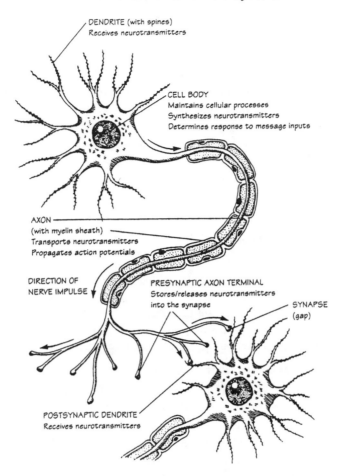

as stomach upset (Perry, 1996). Similarly, messages communicated to and from the brain to the body regulate behavior and thought. For example, the sensory and motor centers of the brain direct the muscles involved in bicycle riding; when rough pavement is encountered, the sensory and motor input from the arms and legs provide information to the brain so that it can signal appropriate changes in motor coordination.

Brain Structures

The brain is composed of nerve cell bodies, fibers (axons and dendrites), glia (supporting and activating cells), and blood vessels. Cerebrospinal fluid flows through a series of open spaces (ventricles). This fluid serves as a shock absorber and helps maintain the shape of the softer brain tissue. In general, the three major anatomical divisions of the brain (spinal cord, brain stem, and forebrain) are successively more complex in organization (Goldberg, 1990). Because many functions of the brain seem to be primarily lodged in particular structural components while also being in interaction with other components, the brain can be characterized as a "modular" entity. Figures 5-7 show the basic structures of the brain from a number of perspectives.

The Cerebral Cortex. This part of the forebrain has two hemispheres (right, left) with four lobes in each hemisphere. The cortex has dense folds that in the adult brain, if stretched flat, would cover about 2.5 square feet. Bulges in these folds are called "gyri" and indentations are called "sulci" or, if deep, "fissures." The four lobes of each hemisphere—frontal, parietal, occipital, and temporal—each have some distinctive functions. In the back of the frontal lobe there is the primary motor cortex, which includes an area that has primary motor control of language (usually more pronounced in the dominant hemisphere). The front (anterior) of the cortex is the primary site of such functions as initiative, drive, ability to control impulses and follow social rules, and ability to perceive and reflect on actions. The somatosensory cortex, located in the parietal lobe, primarily governs sensory processing. The parietal lobe also has an area that controls perception and interpretation of written language. Vision is located primarily in the occipital (back) lobe, while hearing and sound localization are found in the temporal (side) lobe, which also contains an area identified as vital for interpretation of spoken language. As noted earlier, it is believed that an overlap of functions exists in most of these areas; that is, many other parts of the brain are involved in each function. White matter fibers (i.e., axons) within each hemisphere project into subcortical areas, some of which cross the midline to connect the two hemispheres (through the corpus callosum) and some of which provide associations within the same hemisphere. The deeper structures of the forebrain include the lateral ventricle (a C-shaped cavity) and the basal ganglia, which play a role in intentional movement. This area produces the cerebrospinal fluid (CSF), which is transported through the ventricles.

While hemisphere specialization has been identified, there is also much congruence in adult left/right hemisphere responses. Usually, the dominant hemisphere (for most people this is the left hemisphere) is slightly larger, while certain areas in the right hemisphere may be larger (e.g., parietal). The frontal lobe, however, shows little anatomic asymmetry (Lezak, 1995). Research indicates that lateralization of the hemispheres (each having special functions) is most evident in the dominance of speech expression and sequential processing in the left hemisphere, and in the ability to mediate complex, visual stimuli in the right hemisphere. The left hemisphere also may have superiority in processing detailed information, while the right hemisphere may have superiority processing large-scale or global concepts. Right hemisphere capacities for comprehension and seeing relationships, which are necessary for understanding alternative meanings and enjoying jokes, have been found (Lezak, 1995). Normal behavior, however, is a function of the whole brain, with both hemispheres contributing to most activities and emotions. Complex mental tasks, such as reading or mathematics and effective storage and retrieval of memories, need active engagement of both hemispheres.

The Limbic System. Embedded below the cerebral cortex is the area often called the limbic system (or "inner brain"). This area includes the thalamus, which relays and integrates information from sensory systems to the cortex; the hypothalamus, which is the master controller of the autonomic system; the hippocampus, which is involved in

Figure 5
Structures of the Brain: Brain stem and Limbic System

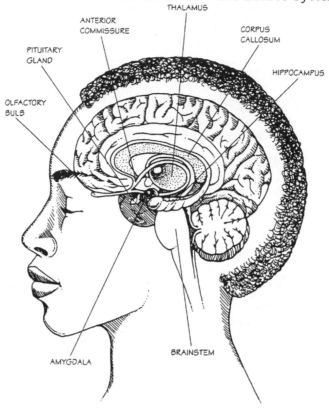

THALAMUS

ANTERIOR
COMMISSURE

CORPUS
CALLOSUM

PITUITARY
GLAND

HIPPOCAMPUS

OLFACTORY
BULB

AMYGDALA

BRAINSTEM

emotional reactions, learning, and memory; and the amygdala, which perceives and interprets emotions, and receives olfactory information. The thalamus also plays a role in alerting processing and response systems, and in regulating higher level brain activity. The hypothalamus, through its control of the autonomic system, governs heart rate, body temperature, appetite and thirst, and sleep/waking cycles through both sympathetic (increasing physical responses) and parasympathetic (decreasing physical responses) processes. Through the pituitary gland, the hypothalamus also governs the endocrine system, which has glands located throughout the body that secrete hormones necessary for growth, sexual development, and other functions. Recent research suggests that these structures are in close interaction with structures in the cortex, and thus they also play a role in higher order thinking.

The Brain Stem. In the hindbrain (brain stem), the cerebellum controls balance, posture, motor coordination, and body space awareness. Recent research indicates that the cerebellum also has some involvement with attention, memory, learning, and touch

(Lezak, 1995). The medulla regulates functions such as breathing, swallowing, blood pressure, and reflex actions like sneezing. Through the medulla run the afferent (*to* higher processing brain centers) and efferent (*from* higher processing brain centers) fibers or axons that connect receptors and effectors in other parts of the body to the central nervous system (CNS). The pons links the cortex with the cerebellum, and has a role in facial expression and eye movement. A network of interconnected nerve cell bodies and fibers form the reticular formation, which holds the reticular activating system (RAS) responsible for controlling wakefulness and alertness.

IMPLICATIONS OF BRAIN FUNCTION/STRUCTURE KNOWLEDGE FOR CHILDHOOD EDUCATION

It is no longer possible for educators to consider knowledge of neurobiological processes as lying outside of their areas of expertise. Scientists are not the only ones who need to know how the neuronal network and its communication processes function, and to understand how the brain's modular structures and primary functions are integrated in complex interactions. While much more remains to be learned before a direct relationship between brain development and particular educational practice can be demonstrated, certain conclusions can be drawn. It is clear that brain development results from the interaction of genes and environmental experiences, that growth and elaboration of the neuronal network during the early years of life are critical to children's

Figure 6
Structures of the Brain: Brain Areas Involved in Conscious Memory

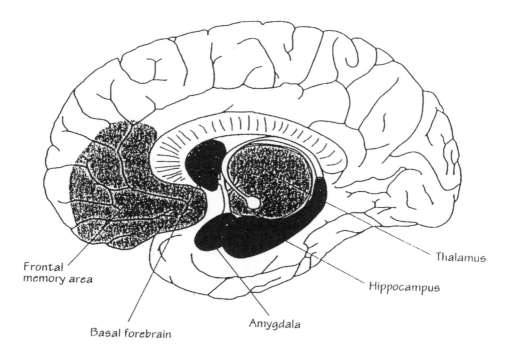

From Mishkin, M., & Appenzeller, T. (1987). The anatomy of memory.
Scientific American, June, 82. Reprinted by permission of artist, Carol Donner.

Figure 7
Structures of the Brain: Language Centers of the Brain

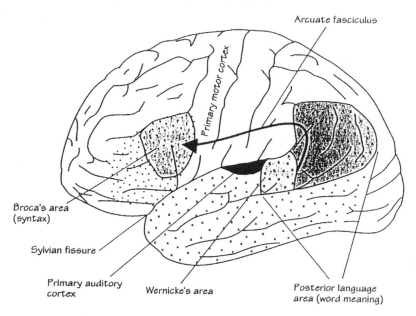

From Damasio & Damasio. (1992). Brain and language. *Scientic American, September,* 90. Reprinted by permission of artist, Carol Donner.

knowledge construction, and that complex interactions among the modular components of the brain influence the efficiency and nature of learning. Moreover, the brain's plasticity (i.e., its flexibility and adaptability) creates multiple opportunities for diverse experiences (or lack of such experiences) to influence its development. In fact, current knowledge suggests that every curriculum and every educational act might be called "brain-based," because every experience (even those not considered educational) has the potential for influencing brain development.

Educators who appreciate the complexity and interconnectedness of children's sensory/motor processing, emotion center monitoring, and higher order thinking can use that knowledge in planning curricula. In particular, their awareness of the similarities and differences that exist among individual brains can enhance their sensitivity to the needs of children whose brains may have experienced biological risk or environmental trauma. Thus, both practicing educators and educators-in-training need to obtain a knowledge base in developmental and functional neuroanatomy if they are to be informed evaluators of brain research for educational practice.

CHAPTER 3

BRAIN GROWTH AND NEUROLOGICAL DEVELOPMENT AND ENVIRONMENTAL EXPERIENCES: PRENATAL TO AGE 3

Because much of recent brain research focused on the prenatal to age 3 period, a relatively clear picture can be given of early brain development and the environmental factors that may influence its direction and health. A number of recently published books provide detailed and neurologically sound descriptions of brain development during prenatal and early years (e.g., Eliot, 1999), offer well-reasoned suggestions for parents (e.g., Ramey & Ramey, 1999), and use brain research to advocate for early intervention in environmental risk conditions (e.g., Shore, 1997). A number of books go beyond the data, however, to make less well-grounded claims for brain-based curricula, and many commercial appeals to parents and educators push "brainy" toys, music, and art materials for infants. It is often difficult for educators and parents to make distinctions between well-reasoned approaches based on current brain research evidence and those approaches that go beyond present evidence in order to support other agendas.

Although there is less specific information about the positive effects of certain environments, research evidence reliably shows that highly negative environmental conditions can result in genetic/environmental interactions that cause harm to the developing fetus and neonate. Research also suggests that a paucity of social-emotional, sensory-motor, and cognitive-language stimulation in the infant and toddler years may retard optimum brain growth and neurological functioning. Evidence is not sufficient to predict specific long-term consequences of poor environments on the anatomy of brain development or the effect of such brain differences on children's learning ability, although a number of hypotheses are being tested.

BRAIN GROWTH AND NEUROLOGICAL DEVELOPMENT DURING THE PRENATAL PERIOD

During prenatal development, the neuronal network and the basic structures of the brain are forming. About 60 percent of human genes are dedicated to brain development (Shore, 1997). The brain is formed from the neural tube, and its development begins shortly after conception. This development progresses "from the neck up," beginning with the brain stem and ending with the cortex. The fetal brain generates many more neurons than will be needed, and they begin forming synaptic connections during the fetal period. The neurons divide and multiply and the axons form basic links primarily from the first few weeks to 6 months of the prenatal period, although most neurons are generated during the second trimester (12 to 20 weeks). This is considered to be the first "critical period" of prenatal development. The neurons migrate during these same time periods, moving from the lateral ventricle toward the skull and forming layers, each built on top of earlier ones, as they move. The fetus begins to show motor and sensory activity very early (about 7 weeks after gestation), and researchers hypothesize that this activity aids early brain development (Hofer, 1988). Other brain areas that begin development early in fetal life are the somatosensory system (touch, pain, and temperature sensitivity); the vestibular system (balance and motion); and the visual, auditory, olfactory, and gustatory senses. Even such higher order systems as language and memory have basic brain configurations designed in the fetal period. (See Eliot, 1999, for precise details on the development of these systems.)

IMPACT OF PRENATAL GENETIC/ENVIRONMENTAL INTERACTION

Prenatal influences on brain development include genetic factors (physiology of egg and sperm; genetic transmission, errors, and mutations) and environmental factors (interuterine environment, maternal illness, and maternal stress and self-care behaviors). Interactions between genetic and environmental factors begin shortly after conception. Many studies indicate that prenatal malnourishment, exposure to teratogens (harmful substances such as radiation, nicotine, alcohol, cocaine), and maternal illness and/or stress can negatively affect specific aspects of early brain development. For example, during the early prenatal period (about 14 days after conception) the phenomenon of cortical cell migration begins, in which the neurons that will form the cortex develop in its deepest layers and travel up "cortical ladders," composed of glial cells, to form the upper sections of the cortex (Rakic, 1995). As the cells proceed up these ladders, they encounter genes that define their purpose and final location. The process works from the bottom up; that is, the first migrating cells stop at the lower levels and each wave of succeeding cells goes above the existing levels to a higher level. By the mid-gestation period, many neurons are involved in this migration process, forming the structures of the cerebral cortex.

If teratogenic substances, such as cocaine or alcohol, are absorbed at the time of cell migration, some of these cells may die and others may not reach their predetermined locations. Exposure to alcohol prenatally may distort this migration process so much that the infant suffers from fetal alcohol syndrome, a developmental disorder associated with intrauterine growth retardation, microcephaly, mental retardation, and craniofacial abnormalities. Illnesses such as influenza also may interfere with the migration process and result in cognitive and emotional impairments. Researchers believe that some neurological disorders such as epilepsy also may be the result of a distortion in the migration process (Rakic, Bourgeois, & Goldman-Rakic, 1994). Other brain development processes may be affected negatively by absorption of teratogens.

Nutrition can be crucial at early stages; a deficiency of folic acid in the first weeks of pregnancy may affect neural tube closure, resulting in spina bifida. General nutritional deficiencies may be more critical at later stages, resulting in infants with low birth weight and smaller head size. Maternal smoking also negatively affects birth weight. Infants with birth weight less than four and one-half pounds have a higher incidence of neurological and mental impairments (Eliot, 1999). A recent study found that effects of very low birth weight (under 750 grams) are even seen at middle-school age, with more low birth weight children evidencing developmental, behavioral, and learning problems (Taylor, Klein, Minich, & Hack, 2000). Maternal stress may affect limbic system development; stress-triggered release of hormones (e.g., corticosteroids, catecholamine) from the hypothalamus-pituitary system may restrict blood flow and interfere with other aspects of the child's brain development.

Although most prenatal research focuses on the negative effects of poor environments, some research identifies the positive learning that may occur prenatally. For example, research indicates that neonates attend more to the sound of their mothers' voices than to other voices, which implies that they have learned to recognize that voice in utero (Lock, 1993). Of course, good nutrition and avoidance of teratogenic substances are also positive influences on growth and development.

Brain Growth and Neurological Development During the First Year

At birth, the brain is still in a relatively undeveloped state. According to Shore (1997), "fully three-quarters of the human brain develops outside the womb, in direct relationship with an external environment" (p. 24). The newborn infant's neurons are almost complete in number (about 100 billion). Although researchers once believed that no new neurons develop postnatally, preliminary evidence suggests that some increases in neurons may occur later in some brain structures (Shankle et al., 1998). In the postnatal period, pruning, the death of unused neurons and synapses, begins in a few areas. This process is related to the "fine-tuning" of the nervous system and its connections. For example, the visual cortex is one of the first to mature, and that area shows extensive synaptogenesis during the first year, while pruning begins to be evident in the second and third years.

The brain continues to grow in spurts postnatally. A brain growth spurt occurs from the third trimester of the prenatal period through the first two years of life, and this represents a second critical or sensitive period in brain development. The weight of the brain increases from about one pound at birth to two pounds by age 1. The increase in the size and weight of the brain is due to an increase in the size of the neurons, elaboration of dendritic elements, myelination of the axons, and an increase in the number and size of glial cells.

Researchers use the newer brain imaging procedures to observe the process of brain development. Much of the information about early brain growth and neurological development comes from the PET studies of Chugani and colleagues (Chugani et al., 1993; Chugani, 1999). These observations of the amount of energy being used by various parts of the brain (seen in the amount of blood flow) at various age levels provide a picture of how the energy patterns change as different areas of the brain develop. For example, Chugani and colleagues (1993) found that the local cerebral metabolic rates for glucose are greater in the sensorimotor areas of the cortex in infants under 4 weeks, when reflexive behaviors dominate. Over time, the metabolic rates of other cerebral areas increase. By 2 or 3 months, glucose usage increases in the parietal and temporal lobes, primary visual cortex, basal ganglia, and cerebellar hemispheres, and these changes coincide with improved visuospatial and visuo-sensorimotor integration and loss of neonatal reflexes. Researchers also report that the frontal areas begin to be active at approximately 6 months. The areas showing increased blood flow after that time are primarily in the frontal cortex and the occipital cortical regions (associated with vision). During this same period, some neonatal reflexes diminish and gradually disappear, possibly as a result of increases in cortical influence.

Chugani and colleagues report a notable increase in activity in much of the frontal lobe by 8 months, corresponding to signs of higher infant cognitive functioning. By 8 months, most infants have sufficient motor control to interact meaningfully with objects and people in their environment, begin to understand language and to express sounds used in that language, and to learn through imitating the actions of others. In the period from 8 months to 12 months, the top (dorsal) and middle (medial) frontal regions show greater activity, which may co-occur with behavior-related cognition, such as stranger anxiety. By age 1, the metabolic activity of the cortex is similar to that found in adult brains.

The somatosensory, vestibular, and motor systems all continue to develop as infants mature, and some of the activities most enjoyed by infants during this age period contribute to further development (Eliot, 1999). For example, infants thrive on being touched, and their ability to reach for and touch people and objects in their environment begins in the first postnatal months. They also love being bounced, swung, turned upside down (all vestibular experiences), as well as exercising their abilities to examine objects by looking, tasting, and making noise with them. Their coordination of such voluntary movements improves as the cerebellum and basal ganglia areas are myelinated.

Social-emotional development also proceeds during this first year as the limbic system matures. Because the amygdala, part of the limbic system, is well-formed at birth, infants can express emotional states at an early age, although these expressions do not appear to be "felt" emotions (Eliot, 1999). The appearance of the social smile at 3-4 months appears to be due more to the myelination of the basal ganglia, which is closely connected to the motor system, than to "sociable feelings." The limbic cortex, where emotions are recognized or "felt," matures during the 6- to 18-month-old period. The expression of infant attachment to caregivers and stranger anxiety are evidence of development in the medial frontal lobe. The two hemispheres alternate growth spurts, and appear to "feel" different emotions; the left side being the site of "good" feelings and the right side the site of "bad" feelings (Dawson et al., 1992). Because emotion and memory are both located in the medial temporal lobe, the development of this area also presumably influences development of young children's memory abilities.

Even before birth, an area between the temporal and parietal lobes (planum temporale) begins to grow larger on the left side of the brain; this is the site of the capacity for understanding of language (Wernicke's area). EEG measures of preterm infants show that by 30 weeks, the two hemispheres of the brain already respond differently to language, with the left hemisphere being specialized for this activity. Newborns are extremely responsive to human speech and infants of six months can discriminate and categorize phonemes from every language. By 1 year, however, they focus on the sounds present in their native language and begin to have difficulty in differentiating similar phonemes if they are from other languages (Kiester, 2001). According to Kuhl, who has researched language for 25 years, "The baby early begins to draw a kind of map of the sounds he hears. . . . That map continues to develop and strengthen. . . . The sounds not heard, the synapses not used, are bypassed and pruned from the brain's network" (Kuhl, cited in Kiester, 2001, p. 15; see Kuhl, 1994). As myelination of the motor nerves that govern speech proceeds, infants begin to babble; by 12 months they can produce most vowel sounds and about half of the consonant sounds. Although environmental factors have a strong influence on language learning, brain research confirms the "nativist" view that the capability for basic language development is "wired" into the anatomical structure of the brain.

BRAIN GROWTH AND NEUROLOGICAL DEVELOPMENT IN YEARS 2 TO 3

During the period from age 1 to 3, the metabolic rate of the brain continues to increase; by age 3, the brain shows about two and one-half times as much activity as the adult brain (Chugani et al., 1993). By age 2, the number of synapses reaches the adult level, and by age 3 the brain has about 1,000 trillion synapses (Shore, 1997). This super-dense synapse condition is twice the density of that present in the adult brain. The young brain also has a higher concentration of neurotransmitters, the communication facilitators of the brain. Brain weight increases as the glial cells provide myelination of the neuronal network, which increases the speed of message transmission. Epstein (1978) hypothesized that this brain growth spurt, which occurs at about 18 months, corresponds to the development of representational thinking such as pretense and language. Indeed, toddler-age children seem to be "biologically primed for learning" (Shore, 1997, p. 21).

Research confirms that the two hemispheres of the brain develop with slightly different patterns of activity. Using the SPECT technique, Chiron and colleagues (1997) studied cerebral blood flow across the childhood age span. They observed greater blood flow in the right hemisphere in 1-year-old children. The amount of blood flow for the hemispheres and for the sensorimotor and parieto-temporal regions increases in the first year and again during the first to third years. Blood flow in sensorimotor areas also increases during the first three years. Chiron and colleagues noted that these changes parallel behavior changes. For example, handedness usually is established between ages 1 and 4 (related to brain hemispheric growth), sensory and motor control is well-established by ages 3 to 4 (related to brain sensorimotor area growth), and perceptual and language growth spurts occur between ages 1 and 3 (related to development in the parieto-temporal areas that are involved in language). (See Figure 7.)

Many parts of the brain are involved in memory; in fact, every neuron carries a memory! Although young infants have implicit memories (existing, but inaccessible) stored in lower brain and mid brain areas, explicit memories (ones able to be expressed) emerge more slowly since they depend on the maturation of the cerebral cortex (Eliot, 1999). Children begin referring to explicit memories when they begin to talk, usually in the early part of the second year. This development of memory and higher intellectual processes begins to be evident as the primary areas for memory activation mature and become myelinated. The hub of memory lies in the medial temporal lobe, which houses the hippocampus, primarily responsible for long-term memory. Other developing areas involved in memory are the medial thalamus and the basal forebrain, both of which store memories, and the prefrontal cortex, which is the site of source memory. By age 3, children are beginning to use their memory consciously and to learn memory strategies such as repetition.

IMPACT OF GENETIC/ENVIRONMENTAL INTERACTION FROM BIRTH TO 3

Researchers believe that much of this early brain development is determined by both genes and experience. Environmental enrichment may increase neuronal complexity, improve brain function, and facilitate recovery from brain injury, and these influences on specific abilities are more pronounced during critical or sensitive periods. In a review of research on the effects of stress on brain development, Nelson and colleagues (Nelson & Bloom, 1997; Nelson & Carver, 1998; Nelson et al., 2000) propose that "plasticity in the developing brain represents a window of opportunity in normal circumstances, and represents a period of vulnerability in adverse circumstances" (Nelson & Carver, 1998, p. 793). For example, Huttenlocher and colleagues (Huttenlocher, 1998; Huttenlocher, Haight, Bryk, & Seltzer, 1991) found that the types of words children spoke and their general vocabulary growth were related to the quantity of words spoken by their mothers. Other researchers report similar findings (e.g., Smolak & Weintraub, 1983; Tomasello, Mannie, & Kruger, 1996). Many studies show that mothers of different socioeconomic classes differ in the amount and complexity of speech directed to their children, and these differences are associated with their children's speech (e.g., Hammer, 1997; Hammer & Weiss, 1999). Hammer suggests that for children under 20 months, genetics play a greater role in speech (with girls acquiring new words faster); after that age, however, the effect of language exposure, rather than genetics, dominates.

Environmental deprivation and/or stress during this early period may alter neuronal, hormonal, and immune systems. These alterations may impair normal development, affecting children's physical, cognitive, and social-emotional development in transient or long-term ways. Although experimental research cannot be done for ethical reasons, some "natural experiments" show correlations between stressful early environments and developmental delays, and children are likely to be more vulnerable to environmental deprivation, stress, or acquired insults during critical or sensitive periods (Perry, 1996). For example, in a study of stress hormone regulation using cortisol samples taken from saliva, Carlson and Earls (1997) found that Romanian infants who were reared in institutions with necessary food, shelter, and clothing, but lacking tactile and social interactions, showed deficits in both physical growth and cognitive development at age 2. These researchers also found a correlation between cortisol levels and performance on cognitive and physical development measures in children reared within the orphanages. Carlson and Earls hypothesized that heightened cortisol levels may indicate greater risk for psychiatric problems (e.g., depression) later in life. While developmental intervention conducted with a group of the Romanian 2- and 3-year-olds accelerated physical growth and mental/motor development in the intervention group, compared to controls, no cognitive differences were found. Cognitive scores for both groups were well below normal. In another study, MRI scans of severely neglected children showed that their brain size was up to 30 percent smaller than controls (Eliot, 1999). Some researchers suggest caution in such interpretations, emphasizing that a number of additional hazards may be present in these non-random samples, thus making cause/effect conclusions questionable (Thompson & Nelson, 2001).

Other researchers have been investigating how specific areas of the brain may be affected by poor or enriched environments. Greenough and colleagues (Greenough, Cohen, & Juraska, 1999) examined how experience regulates neurogenesis within the hippocampus (the site of some types of memory). Without drawing definite conclusions, they suggested that a more enriched environment involving complex learning tasks may encourage the survival of neurons in the dentate gyrus (part of the hippocampus).

Some evidence exists that abused children show a different pattern of electrical activity in the frontal and temporal lobes (in the site of limbic system functions). Brain differences resulting from abuse and neglect may have long lasting social-emotional effects. For example, some children exposed to the severe stress of abuse exhibit strong physiological responses, even to minimal stress conditions, at later ages (Perry, 1996). According to Perry, extreme trauma also may affect brain stem areas that regulate immediate responses related to biological survival, making them "overdevelop," while restricting the development of cortical and limbic areas, which control higher order thinking and emotions. He asserts that the impulsivity, hyperactivity, and poor affect regulation often seen in children from abusive environments may be evidence of this distortion in brain development. The hippocampus also may be atrophied in children who endure abusive situations, resulting in long-term memory deficits (Bremner et al., 1996). In a study of children who had been sexually abused in early childhood (DeBellis et al., 1999), researchers found that at school age, these children had smaller brain volume and larger lateral ventricles, and the corpus callosum was less developed. Moreover, the length of the abuse correlated with the extensiveness of the structural differences in the brain. According to Eliot (1999), such findings show where "the real scars of child abuse and neglect lie: inside children's brains, and especially in the limbic system that defines their personality and governs their emotional future" (p. 325).

Increased cortisol levels, a result of stress, is related to depression in adults, and maternal depression may affect offspring (i.e., depressed mothers may have children with alterations in brain development). In a study of 11- to 17-month-old infants at play with their depressed and non-depressed mothers, Dawson and colleagues (1992) found EEG activity differences in the left and right frontal regions of the brains of these children. Because the left frontal region is more specialized for approach ("good") emotions and the right frontal region is more specialized for withdrawal ("bad") emotions, the researchers expected and found decreased left frontal EEG activity during play and decreased right frontal activity during maternal separation in infants of depressed mothers. The researchers found no significant expressive behavior differences between these groups, although other studies do show some behavior differences in such groups, such as less activity, shorter attention spans, and less motivation to master tasks (Dawson, Hessl, & Frey, 1994).

The identification of structural and functional connections between the emotion and cognitive centers of the brain (e.g., between the amygdala and other parts of the limbic system and certain frontal lobe structures) suggests a close connection between emotion and cognition, with the emotional regulation centers of the brain serving as transmitters and monitors of cerebral functions related to thinking and learning. Greenspan (Greenspan & Lewis, 1999) hypothesizes that infants first learn to discriminate emotions and then learn cognitive categorization; that is, emotional development provides the basis for cognitive development. While this hypothesis needs further research, early evidence suggests that the limbic system (the site of basic emotions) has a mediating influence on higher thought processing.

Brain Structure/Function Relationships to Autistic Spectrum Disorder

One condition associated with alterations in brain development in this early life period is autistic spectrum disorder, which incorporates a range of social skill deficiencies, language delays, and stereotyped or repetitive behaviors. Typically, this disorder has early manifestations and, in some cases, can be diagnosed as early as 2-1/2 to 3 years, when a spurt of development in language and social skills should be evident. Most of the research about the neuropathic physiology of autism is at a very preliminary level. One hypothesis points to a possible dysfunction in the amygdala-centered system (Abell et al., 1999). In a study of adult males with autism, researchers found increased gray matter volume in the amygdala/peri-amygdaloid cortex, middle temporal gyrus, inferior temporal gyrus, and certain regions of the cerebellum. Decreases in gray matter were discovered in the right paracingulate sulcus and left inferior frontal gyrus. They hypothesize that an early disruption in the integrative functions of the amygdala-centered system could account for emotional and social impairments and morphological abnormalities in the brain at later ages. The researchers stress, however, that this explanation is still "highly speculative" (Abell et al., p. 1651).

Other hypotheses under study address relationships between the cerebellum and the frontal lobe. Some researchers (Harris, Courchesne, Townsend, Carper, & Lord, 1999), studying children first diagnosed with autism between the ages of 2 to 6, found that the children's ability to attend to stimuli was related to the size of the cerebellum (i.e., smaller cerebellum, poorer attention). Other studies of children with autism identify a relationship between cerebellar motor functions and attention functions (Allen, Buxton, Wong, & Courchesne, 1997), and an inverse relationship between cerebellum size and frontal lobe size (Carper & Courchesne, 2000). Carper and Courchesne suggest that the developmental link between cerebellum and frontal lobe abnormalities may explain why the impairments in higher order thinking found in individuals with autism are persistent and pervasive.

Other researchers have found delayed maturation of the frontal lobes, elevated serotonin, and general brain enlargement as more common in individuals with autism. Dawson and colleagues (Dawson, Meltzoff, Osterling, & Rinaldi, 1998) examined neuropsychological correlates of autistic symptoms in young children and found that the severity of their behaviors (which included deficits in symbolic play) are also related to tasks involving the medial temporal lobes of the brain. Piven (1997), however, in a review of hypothetical causes of autism, states that as yet "there is no obvious single brain structure or system that can be singled out as defective in autism" (p. 709). Although the "practitioner" literature offers many environmentally based hypotheses for autism spectrum disorders (e.g., nutrition, immunizations), little or no research is available on most hypothesized genetic/environment interactional effects. Also, much of the brain structure/function research used older individuals as subjects, and it is not clear if these relationships were present in early brain development. Piven and O'Leary (1997) suggest that "clarification of the timing of brain enlargement in autism through longitudinal imaging studies is warranted" (p. 318). This is also the case for other structural anomalies found in adults with autism. Piven and O'Leary do predict that future neuroimaging research will advance understanding of this condition.

IMPLICATIONS OF BRAIN RESEARCH FOR CHILDHOOD EDUCATION

While many questions remain to be answered, brain research on prenatal, neonatal, infant, and toddler years suggests a number of important implications for practice.

Implications for the Prenatal Period

Because brain research clearly indicates that the prenatal environment affects optimum brain development, one of the first implications of this research is that of "do no harm" (Shore, 1997). It is essential that professionals communicate the need for early prenatal care. During the fetal stage, excellent maternal nutrition and avoidance of teratogens are essential for healthy brain development (Thompson & Nelson, 2001). Unfortunately, many women still do not have optimum prenatal care and their children may be more at risk for brain development problems. Although medical professionals are most involved in ensuring such care, educarers providing out-of-home care and education for infants and toddlers (Bergen, Reid, & Torelli, 2001) often have unique, informal opportunities to explain to parents how the brain develops in utero and to stress the importance of good prenatal care. If educarers share this information routinely, then parents will have valuable knowledge to guide them during subsequent pregnancies. It is especially important to communicate this message to teen parents, who may be less likely to seek early prenatal care. Educators of older children, especially those who may be teaching children who come from conditions of environmental risk, also should find ways to communicate information about pregnancy health to parents, collaborating with agencies that provide the care needed to promote healthy prenatal development and relieve parental stress. School policy should be set to routinely provide such information and offer links to support services that give assistance. Both Early Head Start and Early Start programs provide prenatal education and referral assistance, for example, and these programs are often linked to educational and health agencies.

Implications for the Birth to Age 3 Period

In relation to public policy, Puckett, Marshall, and Davis (1999) caution that the use of information from brain research holds both promise and peril. Resultant public policies may improve health, nutrition, care, and educational opportunities for young children, or may be merely superficial (like those instituted in Georgia and Florida that focus on providing classical music to infants and toddlers). Six primary implications for educarers can be drawn from current brain research:

1)   Because research indicates close emotion/cognition connections in brain structure and functions, early environments that foster emotional safety and promote warm adult-child social interactions appear to be most likely to facilitate young children's social-emotional and cognitive development (Shore, 1997). Environments that lack positive social-emotional elements and that promote high levels of stress in young children should be avoided. Therefore, educarers need to provide emotionally safe environments in their programs, and to work with parents to help them provide such environments as well. While safe environments must be healthful ones, free of noxious conditions and potential hazards, such measures are not sufficient for providing emotional safety. The environment also must have consistent educarers who are knowledgeable about early development, trustworthy in their responsiveness and nurturance, and able to encourage child autonomy in meeting age-appropriate challenges. The best environment is a "yes/yes/no" one, in which many actions are permitted and supported by educarers and only a few are prohibited (Bergen, Smith, & O'Neill, 1989).

2)   Researchers believe milestones in young children's development (e.g., motor control advances, beginning language) co-occur with significant changes in brain structure and/or function. Although the research findings are still preliminary, the milestones noted in brain development appear to be linked to milestones (often called stages or levels) in cognitive, emotional, language, physical, and social behavior. These findings support much of what theorists such as Piaget (1952) and others have observed. Therefore, educarers can assume that when they encourage children's active manipulation of objects, scaffold children's mastery of specific developmental milestones, and provide opportunities for varied experiences, they are also facilitating children's brain development.

3)   There has been an exponential increase in the number of educare environments for very young children. Many of these programs begin shortly after the neonatal period, and they range in quality from ones that are adequately staffed with educarers who are knowledgeable about developmental needs of very young children to ones that have minimal staffing ratios and staff qualifications. Many children are in out-of-home care with relatives and family care providers, whose qualifications also are wide ranging. The Romanian evidence that pervasive exposure to extremely poor environmental quality has a negative relationship to the quantity and types of synaptic connections is congruent with research findings showing that high-quality child care programs (i.e., high adult-to-child ratios, small class size, nurturing and active play environments) have positive effects on young children's development (CQO Study Team, 1995; National Institutes of Child Health and Human Development [NICHD], 1999). This research also shows that children from high-risk family environments (e.g., neglectful/abusive or low in socioeconomic level) seem to benefit most from high-quality child care environments. Because of genetic/environment interaction, children will still show

individual differences in behavior (and presumably in brain organization and development). In light of brain research findings, however, childhood education proponents need to be vocal advocates for programs of high quality for all very young children.

4) Although there is no specifically confirmed research evidence, it is likely that there is a "threshold" of environmental opportunity that is sufficient for brain development to occur without difficulty. The type of social and physical environment provided in high-quality programs (and in the majority of homes) is probably sufficient for most children, even those from high-risk backgrounds, without the use of specifically designated "brain-based" activities. For children who have had traumatic prenatal environments and/or substandard care during their first years of life, however, brain research implies that educarers may need to pay rigorous attention to the specific environments they provide for those children. Evidence exists that intensive early intervention for children in such circumstances has long-term positive effects (Campbell & Ramey, 1994).

5) While some periods of brain development seem to be critical or sensitive, the brain's plasticity at early ages suggests that brain development can be furthered if children experience an enriched environment at later ages (Thompson & Nelson, 2001). If brain development research is better able to pinpoint the brain anatomy effects of early negative environmental conditions, the therapeutic aspects of out-of-home high-quality environments will gain even more importance. Children with early identified disabilities (e.g., Down syndrome, autistic spectrum disorder) may especially benefit from environments and activities that enhance the growth of certain brain areas. Especially in regard to autism, many specific education/training practices are being promoted by various groups; at the present time, however, the brain research evidence is so limited that no claims being made for any of these intensive "brain-based" programs are supportable. Future findings may enable early intervention proponents to be more precise about why and how various interventions are effective than they can be at the present time.

6) Because parents are usually the primary caregivers during the years when biological/environmental interaction influences on brain development are most crucial, their influence on the course of such development is extensive. Educarers of infants and toddlers should view parent involvement and education as crucial elements of their childhood education programs. Educarers can offer valuable help to parents who are struggling to sort through conflicting advice about what toys or experiences they should provide for their children's early education.

CHAPTER 4
BRAIN GROWTH AND NEUROLOGICAL DEVELOPMENT AND ENVIRONMENTAL EXPERIENCES: AGES 3 TO 8

The early part of the 3 to 8 age period continues the phase of rapid brain growth and associated major environmental vulnerability, especially in relation to development of language and intellectual systems. Some preliminary, but controversial, evidence suggests that neuron generation may continue, with the number of cortical neurons possibly doubling between age 15 months and 6 years (Shankle et al., 1998). From ages 3 to 6, synaptogenesis (development of new synapses) continues rapidly; by age 4, cerebral metabolic rates of glucose utilization are twice that of normal adult levels (Chugani et al., 1993). Cerebral size levels off during this age period (Giedd et al., 1996). Despite minimal research on anatomical brain development of children older than 6, existing evidence indicates that synaptogenesis, as measured by glucose metabolic rates, continues to occur throughout the 6 to 8 age period (Chugani et al., 1993). Myelination also continues in particular brain areas (e.g., in portions of the limbic system), especially during the 3 to 6 age period (Gibson, 1991).

BRAIN GROWTH AND NEUROLOGICAL DEVELOPMENT DURING THE 3-8 AGE PERIOD

Chiron and colleagues (1997) found change points in cerebral blood flow levels during the 3-5 age period, with a change beginning at age 3 for sensorimotor areas, at age 3 for parieto-temporal regions, and at age 5 for hemispheres; this finding signals further refinements in fine motor, sensory-gross motor, memory, and language skills. Thompson and colleagues (Thompson et al., 2000) scanned brain growth patterns, over a four-year period, of children ages 3-15, and they report that the 3-6 age period shows the fastest growth rates in the frontal networks that regulate planning of new actions. Source memory, which is awareness of where and when something was learned, emerges only in the latter part of this age period and coincides with maturation of the frontal lobe (Eliot, 1999).

Due to the paucity of brain development research focusing on children older than age 6, little information exists about later developments in the anatomy of brain structures. Also, few studies examine the relationship between brain development and behavior after age 6. Because cognitive neuroscience is so young, Bruer (1999) comments, "We know relatively little about learning, thinking, and remembering at the level of brain areas, neural circuits, or synapses; we know very little about how the brain thinks, remembers, and learns" (p. 650).

Theoretical relationships are being proposed, however. For example, Fischer and Rose (1998) have related Fischer's neo-Piagetian theory of levels of cognitive development to the emerging evidence on cortical growth cycles. Fischer's theory hypothesizes four nested developmental cycles or levels: reflexes (3 to 11 weeks), actions (3-4 months to 11-13 months), representations (2 years to 7 years), and abstractions (10 years to 20 years). Within each cycle are three tiers: single competencies develop, mapping of these competencies then occurs, and, finally, competency systems emerge. Fischer and Rose suggest that new discoveries about brain functioning have led to the first evidence of "parallels of these cortical cycles with the cognitive developmental cycles for levels and tiers" (p. 58). As evidence, they cite Thatcher's (1994) EEG studies that show systematic spurts at the age periods discussed by Fischer. The studies support the view that these cycles follow a definite re-organizational pattern in the brain (Thatcher, 1994, cited in Fischer & Rose, 1998). As yet, researchers do not have sufficient empirical validation of these theoretical relationships; however, this hypothesis is a promising area for further study.

A few studies focus on the relationship of brain activity to temperament and behavior in the 3 to 5 age period. For example, Fox and colleagues (Fox et al., 1995; Fox, Schmidt, Calkins, & Rubin, 1996) studied frontal lobe activity during preschoolers' play, and findings indicate that highly social children with right frontal EEG asymmetry were more likely to have externalizing problems than highly social children with left frontal EEG asymmetry. Furthermore, shy children with increased right frontal EEG asymmetry showed more internalizing problems than did those with left frontal EEG asymmetry. Fox and colleagues proposed that many cognitive processes may be mediated by areas within the frontal lobe, and that children with greater left frontal asymmetry may be better prepared to regulate affective arousal. No conclusions can be reached without confirming studies, however.

Memory and intellectual processes, such as problem solving, gain in speed and efficiency during this age period. Scientists use measures of electrical transmission within the brain (ERPs) to study such processing speed. With older subjects, they compare individuals' processing rates with their scores on intelligence tests. Some studies of children's processing show that their reaction and inspection times grow shorter and performance on cognitive tests grows faster as their age increases. Most such studies examine children older than 5, and show that the largest gains in speed occur between ages 5 and 11 (Hale, 1990). Another ERP feature is the P300 wave, which does not show up unambiguously until age 4 or 5 and does not reach full amplitude and speed until adolescence (Eliot, 1999). In adults, this wave occurs about 300 milliseconds after a stimulus starts, and may be related to awareness of mental experiences. By age 6 or 7, children begin to achieve adult-level performance on tasks requiring attention and inhibition of impulses; from age 4 to 8, P300 responses increase rapidly (McIsaac & Polick, 1992). These brain changes are concurrent with the period Piaget (1952) identified as the stage of concrete operational thought, in which children demonstrate logical reasoning about conservation of matter.

Brain imaging experiments demonstrate that less brain energy (glucose) is burned as tasks are mastered (Haier et al., 1992). As noted earlier, children process more slowly but use more energy than adults. At age 4, glucose use is twice that of adults and then gradually declines through middle childhood and adolescence—the same time that the pruning process is occurring (Chugani et al., 1993). Children ages 7 to 14 still activate a larger brain area than adults use when carrying out discrimination tasks (Haier et al., 1992).

The slow maturation of the frontal lobe also appears to affect children's higher order cognitive abilities. Synaptic density in the frontal lobe peaks at about 7 years, as compared with peaking at 1 year in the visual cortex (Eliot, 1999). The levels of dopamine, a neurotransmitter that affects brain circuits, rise only gradually in the frontal lobe during this age period, and myelination of the frontal lobe continues until early adulthood.

By age 6, however, individual brain differences may be relatively stable. For example, stable differences might be seen in children's brain organization that are reflected in such skills as phonological awareness, vocabulary extent, and/or later reading and math abilities (Fletcher et al., 1994; Molfese, Molfese, & Espy, 1999). Brain activation areas in children ages 6 to 8 should be studied to confirm such specific hypotheses. More generally, the age period from 3 to 8 may involve more individualization of brain structures and functions as children interact with environmental experiences. Although researchers debate whether the brain's plasticity can later overcome a lack of growth-enhancing experiences at critical or sensitive time periods, the opportunities for expansion of the synaptic system do appear to be more limited by the end of this age period.

As Eliot (1999) states,

All of the essential refinements in brain wiring—dendritic growth, spine formation, synapse selection, and even myelination—can be influenced by a child's experience. But once a given brain region has passed the refinement stage, its critical period has ended, and the opportunity to rewire it is significantly limited. Thus the critical periods for basic sensory abilities, like vision and hearing, end much earlier than those for more complex skills, like language and emotion, whose underlying neural circuits prune their synapses and myelinate their axons over most of childhood. Nonetheless, all critical periods probably begin within the first four years of life, when the synaptic tide turns from waxing to waning in all brain areas. (p. 38)

It is during this age period that learning disabilities and attention deficit disorders are often diagnosed. Most of the evidence relating these problems to brain functioning comes from neuropsychological evaluations, rather than from brain imaging research.

RELATIONSHIP OF BRAIN STRUCTURE/FUNCTION TO LEARNING DISABILITIES AND ATTENTION DEFICIT/HYPERACTIVITY DISORDERS

Researchers hypothesize that learning disabilities and attention deficit/hyperactivity disorders are brain-related. Typically, learning disabilities (especially dyslexia) and attention deficit/hyperactivity disorders are diagnosed during the 5 to 8 age period.

Few brain imaging studies have been conducted, however. Neuropsychological studies are critical in understanding early cognitive markers of learning disabilities. For example, researchers found that phonological awareness and vocabulary at kindergarten predict long-term school performance in reading and math (Fletcher et al., 1994; Hart & Risley, 1995; Molfese, Molfese, & Espy, 1999; Morrison, Alberts, & Griffiths, 1997). Hart and Risley (1995) found that vocabulary differences at age 2 predicted verbal IQ and language differences at age 5, and Morrison and colleagues (1997) found that vocabulary at age 5 predicts 3rd-grade reading and math ability. Fletcher and colleagues (1994) reported that phonological decoding deficits at age 5 characterize poor readers, regardless of IQ or IQ achievement discrepancy, and predict persistent reading problems relative to good readers.

Some evidence indicates that dyslexia (impairment of ability to read) has a genetic component (Pennington, 1995), because approximately 40 percent of dyslexic children have parents and/or siblings with the syndrome. Some studies show atypical cortical patterns of blood flow in the left temporal and parietal regions of reading-disabled individuals who are performing literacy tasks (Flowers, Wood, & Naylor, 1991; Wood, Flowers, & Buchsbaum, 1991), and differences in brain metabolic rates in the medial temporal lobe in dyslexic, as compared to nondyslexic, adults (Hagman et al., 1992). Recent fMRI findings by Shaywitz and colleagues (1998) show differing activation patterns in the brain during performance of phonological tasks between these groups. Differences also may be present in the cortical vision systems (Eden et al., 1996). Zeffiro and Eden (2000) indicate that a number of neuroimaging studies of reading and early sensory processing implicate sites in the left hemisphere (e.g., occipitotemporal sulcus, posterior superior temporal gyrus, inferior parietal cortex). While these are only early findings, the evidence suggests that "dyslexia is a complex, multifaceted, brain-based disorder . . . that . . . is not reducible to a mere discrepancy between ability and achievement" (Meyer, 2000, p. 325). As with brain-autism relationships in the early years, no longitudinal imaging studies of brain development from ages 3 to 8 have focused on children who might be at risk for learning disabilities.

Recent brain research also includes exploration of brain growth and neurological development differences in young children with attention deficit/hyperactivity disorder (ADHD). There appears to be a genetic component, and researchers exploring possible gene variants in children with ADHD suggest that the variant DRD4, which codes for a dopamine receptor, may interfere with biochemical messages (LaHoste et al., 1996). Other researchers are investigating whether an abnormality in the maturation and development of brain areas is associated with the motor cortex. Their research employs transcranial magnetic stimulation to identify any delay in the maturation of motor inhibition as compared to typically developing children (Connolly, Brown, & Bassett, 1968; Denckla, 1974). The pattern of neuropsychological behavior in ADHD children seems to be related to executive functions and working memory, which are sited in the frontal lobe; some neuroimaging studies implicate frontosubcortical pathways, which are rich in catecholamines—components of the drugs used in treating ADHD (Faraone & Biederman, 1998). Panksepp (1998) cites Barkley's (1997) findings of less mature frontal lobe development in children with ADHD, and theorizes that since this lobe is primarily responsible for inhibition of action, planning, and conceptualization of complex tasks, the longer period of active rough and tumble play, which these young children seem to need, may facilitate their frontal lobe development. He suggests that ADHD-type behavior may signal that these children need longer periods and more extensive levels of such play. He speculates that drugs for ADHD, which inhibit activity and make children passive, may actually inhibit their frontal lobe development. Given the number of young children being diagnosed with ADHD and treated with such drugs, more research on this hypothesis must be done. This need becomes especially urgent as playground researchers find that children now have fewer opportunities for active recess play at school (Pellegrini & Bjorklund, 1996).

IMPACT OF GENETIC/ENVIRONMENTAL INTERACTION INFLUENCES

Although there are fewer studies of the impact of environment on brain development during this age period, some studies have found linkages between learning tasks and certain areas of the brain.

For example, Fiez (1996) cites a multitude of studies focusing on cerebellar contributions to learning and cognition. He suggests that difficult, novel tasks such as reading new words or generating verbs from nouns, which require trial and error at first and then become easier with practice, may require actions in the cerebellum. Fiez notes that as research continues, understanding of the cerebellum (and other parts of the brain) grows, but only minimal application possibilities for education can be presently identified.

Schooling itself appears to have an effect on memory skills and cognitive development, however, perhaps because children develop "meta" strategies that enable them to think about their learning abilities and to channel their learning (Kail, 1990). One reason children's memories improve may be because they have learned to apply some memory strategies, and this improves the efficiency of the brain's memory functions. No studies as yet specifically measure brain changes as a result of schooling. Neuroscience findings at this time are not able to address the effects of specific educational strategies on brain development, because research has not focused on the effects of such specific strategies. Bruer (1999) states that most advice about educational strategies related to brain development "originated in the popular press and in advocacy documents. It is an instance where neuroscientists have speculated about the implications of their work for education and where educators have uncritically embraced that speculation" (p. 653).

IMPLICATIONS FOR CHILDHOOD EDUCATION

Because research on brain development after age 5 is so sparse, the implications for childhood education in this age period are highly speculative. Some authors stress the importance of possible brain/cognition relationships and give educational suggestions based on their hypotheses. For example, Fischer and Rose (1998) suggest educators work at lower as well as higher levels of children's cognitive functioning, appreciate the plasticity and cyclical nature of cognitive/brain growth by helping children relearn/rework concepts at each level, provide contextual support for high-level functioning, and accept that normal functioning may not always be at optimal levels. Others give recommendations for specific strategies based on theoretical perspectives (e.g., whole language, cooperative learning, left/right brain teaching). Bruer (1999) objects to recommending any specific educational practices based on brain research, however, because there has been no targeted research confirming these relationships. He believes that much of the advice presently being given to educators goes beyond the data. For example, he states that most suggestions given to educators about teaching to the left or right brain misinterpret the information about brain hemisphere specialization, making it appear much more specifically localized, while research really shows that both hemispheres are involved in most tasks. He also questions the rigid use of the terms "critical" or "sensitive periods," saying that most abilities are characterized by growth over long periods of time. He adds that "neuroscientists have little idea of how experience before puberty affects either the timing or the extent of synaptic elimination" (p. 656). Because of these conflicting views on the implications of brain research for education, only limited and general implications can be stated.

1)   Educators working with children ages 3 to 8 may want to emphasize the following in their curricula. First, they can provide an environment with many opportunities for exercising social-emotional, physical-sensory-motor, and language-cognition abilities, in the hope that this will promote the development of new synaptic connections. Second, they can encourage mastery experiences that use children's emerging skills in repetitive games and in concentrated "real-world" tasks. Having many opportunities to use skills appears to strengthen existing synaptic connections in those basic learning areas that are important for overall educational success (e.g., language, memory). Third, they can encourage individual children to practice using their particular specialized skills and talents so that the synaptic connections related to these abilities will be strengthened (e.g., artistic or mathematical talent, interest in history or science). Until the pruning process is better understood, the most promising role for educators may be to offer educational experiences that give children opportunities to develop a plethora of synapses, gain strongly developed synaptic connections in areas basic to overall learning success, and be able to exercise all of their unique abilities. Until more is known about the specific effects of education on the brain's structures and functions, a curriculum that supports all three of these ways to support synaptogenesis is probably best.

2)   Educators also should try to extend the abilities of both boys and girls, even while acknowledging possible small differences in brain structures and processing activities. The evidence of gender differences in children's brains is minimal at present, and most of it is difficult to interpret. While more evidence of gender differences can be found in adult brains, these are likely to be a result of genetic/environment interactions. Moreover, most of this research shows that while males and females may differ on a particular dimension, an overlapping range exists on all measured dimensions, with many males and females performing similarly. Until more is known about the influence of genetic/environment interactions on brain development, a non-stereotypic view that fosters optimum brain development for both genders is best. That is, educators should avoid gender-stereotyped "left-brained" or "right-brained" curriculum approaches.

3)   Advocacy for positive, emotionally safe environments and high-quality edu-

cational experiences for all children at this age level is clearly warranted, given the fact that, although the specifics of positive environmental effects on brain development are not clear, the negative effects of some types of extremely poor environments are already documented by brain research (Perry, 1996). Because of greater research interest in the brain structure and functional abnormalities of children with disabilities, it is likely that more information on educational strategies will be available for these children before much evidence is available on promoting optimum educational practices for typically developing children. Because most educators now work in inclusive environments, however, they need to stay informed about what the latest brain research suggests for working with children with disabilities.

4)   Research on the relationship between early phonological and vocabulary skills and later risks for learning disabilities suggests that educators and parents should actively foster language abilities, including phonological awareness and vocabulary development. Early, accurate diagnosis and intervention for children with delays in these areas (at least by age 5-7) are preferred over a "wait and see" approach. Research suggests that learning disabilities can have a lifelong impact; although children may "outgrow" one problem, they may "grow" into another. For example, they may progress from having poor phonological awareness to becoming non-readers to becoming slow readers in adolescence. Unfortunately, current research in this area is correlational rather than demonstrating cause/effect. That is, a relationship between these conditions is clear, but no direct experimental evidence exists that providing early activities to increase phonological awareness will result in good reading skills at later ages. A sufficient body of research exists, however, to warrant early attention to preventing vocabulary and phonological deficits in young children, since such deficits are related to later reading problems.

5)   Although some research is giving clues to genetic and brain-related causes of ADHD, there are no precise studies identifying causal factors or investigating the long-term effects of drugs that inhibit motor behavior on brain growth and neurological development. It may be that some children need this higher level of motor activity to further the development of their motor and frontal lobe functions. In light of the debate about drug treatment options, educators can at least be sure that children are not required to inhibit motor activity so stringently that they lose whatever benefits such activity may provide for motor and frontal lobe maturation. It is likely that children diagnosed with ADHD may have a delay in maturation of these areas. Thus, practices such as omitting recess time or requiring long periods of intense concentration without motor breaks may have implications for the brain maturation of such children. Further suggestions for educators may be forthcoming as this research progresses.

CHAPTER 5

Brain Growth and Neurological Development and Environmental Experiences: Ages 8 to 14

A major brain development activity that begins in earnest at age 8 or 9 and continues until the late teens is synaptic pruning. Presumably, those synapses that have been less used are eliminated and those that were used most frequently are maintained. However, few facts are known about how this process occurs. Eliot (1999) comments,

> It would be hard to overstate the importance of synaptic refinement to a child's developmental potential. The initial wiring of a particular brain region (the period of synapse overproduction) marks the onset of a particular ability, such as vision in the first few months and language in the second year. But it is the prolonged pruning period that fixes the overall quality of that ability, because this is when experience—translated into neural activity—decides which connections will be preserved and, consequently, how the brain will be permanently wired for certain ways of thinking, perceiving, and acting. As long as an excess number of synapses are present, the brain remains maximally plastic and can develop in a variety of ways. But once those excess synapses are gone, the critical period is over, and it must make do with its existing circuitry; there's no trading up for a faster computer. (p. 38)

Brain Growth and Neurological Development During the 8-14 Age Period

While synaptogenesis begins to decrease during this age period, myelination continues to be active at least through the first decade. Myelination goes on even longer in certain parts of the brain, such as the area around the parahippocampal gyrus, where there is a doubling in the extent of myelination relative to brain weight (Benes, Turtle, Khan, & Farol, 1994; Locke & Yakovlev, 1965). In the study of the relationship between glucose use and the functioning of neuroanatomic structures (Chugani et al., 1993), the 1CMRGlc rates began a slow decline beginning around age 9 and reached adult rates by 20 years. Thus, the primary pruning period appears to be about as long as the primary synaptogenesis period. Thompson and Nelson provide a schematic view of the maturation patterns of various brain structures, showing that this process extends into adolescence (see Figure 8).

Speed and efficiency of memory continues to develop during this age period. Nelson et al. (2000), who studied spatial working memory in children 8 to 11.6 years, found that it was localized primarily in the middle frontal gyrus, in the superior frontal gyrus, and in the left anterior cingulate (areas in the frontal lobe). The children's accuracy of

Figure 8
Trends in Brain Development

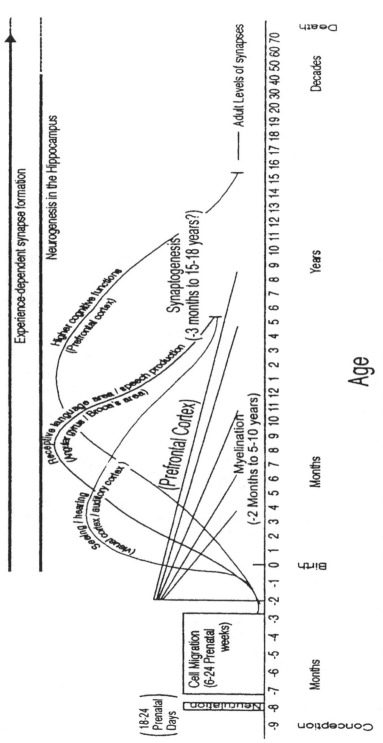

Note. This graph illustrates the importance of prenatal events, such as the formation of the neural tube (neurulation) and cell migration; critical aspects of synapse formation and myelination beyond age three; and the formation of synapses based on experience, as well as neurogenesis in a key region of the hippocampus (the dentate gyrus), throughout much of life.

From Thompson, R. A., & Nelson, C. A. (2001). Developmental science and the media: Early brain development. *American Psychologist*, *56*(1), 5-15. Copyright © 2001 by the American Psychological Association. Reprinted with permission.

memory was similar to that of healthy adults, with like activation in the posteriorparietal region and dorsal aspects of the frontal cortex. Using electrophysiological markers of cortical change, Travis (1998) looked at speed of processing and executive functioning in children 9 and older, finding them to be associated with electrophysiological markers. The researcher urged caution in interpreting these findings, however. Through PET scans during a thumb-to-finger tapping activity, differences in activation of motor regions were found between adults and children age 9 (Mueller et al., 1998). Adults showed less activation in the temporal lobe and angular and posterior gyri, but they had an increase in blood flow in the cerebellum. The researchers concluded that once a task (such as the thumb-to-finger tapping activity) is learned and automated within the brain, the higher brain centers are less involved.

As the prefrontal cortex matures, critical thinking and problem-solving abilities become more evident, and the regulation of emotional states and judgments greatly improves. In the brain growth mapping study of Thompson and colleagues (Thompson et al., 2000), the researchers found that in the years before puberty there was a peak growth rate in the fibers innervating association and language cortical areas, as well as extensive growth of part of the corpus callosum. These findings suggest that a major increase in the richness of communication networks occurs as children enter adolescence. In a study by Kwon and Lawson (2000), maturation of the prefrontal lobes in early adolescence correlated with scientific reasoning ability and showed great improvement by age 15. The researchers state that such reasoning requires the ability to inhibit task-irrelevant information and represent task-relevant information. The maturation rate of certain brain areas may differ in boys and girls. For example, Warrick and Naglieri (1993) found that girls were better at attention tasks in 3rd grade and in planning tasks in 6th grade, but that these differences between boys and girls faded by 9th grade. Thus, functions such as planning, rehearsing future actions, predicting, and controlling emotion with logical thought (through cortex/limbic system connections) all develop greatly in late childhood, although this maturational process continues through adolescence (Sylwester, 1995). Thompson and Nelson (2001) conclude

The brain regions most relevant to higher cognition, including reasoning and problem solving, self-regulation, personality, and strategic functioning, have a maturational course extending into adolescence, consistent with the research evidence (and everyday observation) of how significantly children develop during this period in their thinking, social functioning, self-control, and other capacities. (p. 10)

IMPACT OF GENETIC/ENVIRONMENTAL INTERACTION INFLUENCES

A few studies raise some interesting questions about genetic/environmental interactions during this age range. Giedd and colleagues (1997) examined the relationship between age, gender, and brain morphometry in older children (mean age 11.6). They found age-related decreases in ventricular volume, but gave no explanation for that finding. (Unlike neurons, glial cells, which contribute to ventricular volume, undergo a constant cycle of proliferation and cell death, and by this age glial cells outnumber neurons.) The relationship between glial cell volume and the size, number, or activity of neurons is poorly understood, however. Giedd and colleagues reported that male brains were larger. In their longitudinal study of children ages 4-18, these researchers later reported a number of brain areas that differed in size between males and females. For example, males showed an increase in lateral ventricular volume after age 11 and increases in the amygdala, whereas hippocampal volume increased more in females. The researchers did not hypothesize about potential environmental factors that may influence such differences, but they stated, "given the myriad of factors that determine brain structure size, . . . size difference should not be interpreted as imparting any sort of functional advantage or disadvantage" (p. 1195).

Maturational differences may have implications for types and timing of instruction children receive. Studying this age period, Tallal and colleagues (1996) found that during language training, cortical reorganization occurred in the language areas of the brain. Although proponents of various educational practices recommend particular teaching strategies to enhance brain development, few studies of how specific educational interventions affect brain development have been conducted. Memory, problem solving, and metacognitive skills do appear to continue being influenced by the schooling experience. Although the evidence is behavioral and correlational (that is, showing relationships but not causality), research shows that people with more years of schooling perform better on many memory and problem-solving tasks. The ability to use memory deliberately and to learn memory strategies that can be consciously used appear to have both a brain maturation component and an environmental component, being influenced by school experiences (Kail, 1990). For example, in a review of using the LOGO programming language to solve problems, Clements and Sarama (1997) found increases in children's metacognition; the children were more able to understand their own thinking processes and to find the flaws in their thinking when the program did not respond as expected. The studies they describe, however, did not relate these results to brain structural changes.

Brain Injury and Its Relationship to Childhood Development

Traumatic brain injury (TBI) is not rare among children. Epidemiological surveys indicate that admissions for TBI include 185 to 230 cases per 100,000 children below age 15. Of these cases, 10-15 percent involve moderate to severe injury (Klaus, 1995). Although TBI can occur at an earlier age (e.g., shaking of infants), it often occurs between ages 8 and 14 when children are more involved in risk-taking activities. Motor vehicle accidents in which the child is a passenger, pedestrian, or bicyclist are the main cause of TBI for young school-age children. As they grow older, brain trauma as a result of recreation and sport injuries increases (e.g., football, skating).

There may be many different cognitive and behavioral outcomes of TBI, depending on the nature of the injury in combination with multiple other factors (e.g., child age, premorbid behavioral or cognitive weaknesses). For example, a common type of brain injury that occurs during vehicle accidents is called a contre-coup injury. This occurs when a child's head strikes the inside of the car; the brain hits the skull at the point of impact and then bounces back to the opposite side of the skull. Contusion or bruising of brain matter can occur on the opposite side of the brain. The rotational forces stretch and tear axons, many of which will be permanently damaged and some of which will die. This damage is not localized to one area, and may result in bleeding within the brain due to disruption of blood vessels. Swelling also may occur, which disrupts blood flow and compresses brain tissue. Thus, the damage due to such an injury can affect multiple brain regions and functions.

Children who sustain a TBI may have at least transient cognitive impairments, such as deficits in intelligence, memory, processing speed, attention, and language and psychomotor skills. Behavioral consequences include poor impulse control and unmanageability, anxiety, irritability, agitation, confusion, loss of spontaneity, lack of insight, and affective disturbances. Researchers who have followed children with varying degrees of TBI over time have found behavioral changes and emerging behavioral problems to be common (e.g., Rutter et al., 1980). Furthermore, family burden and functioning prior to and after the injury are related to behavioral and cognitive outcomes in the child (e.g., Taylor et al., 1995).

Although children usually show a rapid recovery from TBI during the first 6 months, children with moderate or severe injuries may continue to exhibit cognitive, behavioral, physical, and sensory symptoms. Furthermore, recovery may never be complete. TBI may affect future development through: 1) changes in course and rate of development, 2) reduction in ultimate level of skill achievement, 3) loss of previously attained skills, and 4) negative effects on development of new skills (Mira, Tucker, & Tyler, 1992). In addition, when children below age 15 experience one TBI, they are twice as likely to sustain another such injury than are children in general. This may be because they are likely to exhibit impulsiveness, poor judgment and safety awareness, or balance and coordination difficulties, as a result of the first injury. Furthermore, they are often at risk for psychosocial stressors such as change in the family roles after the accident, loss of a family member, change in friendships, and loss of independence.

IMPLICATIONS FOR CHILDHOOD EDUCATION

Although the brain research base is limited at this age level, a number of implications might be derived from existing research, as follows:

1)   It is important for educators of children ages 8-14 to keep in mind that this is a period of significant brain development. The brain is undergoing a reorganization that eventually will result in relatively stable structures and functions. Although it is presently not known exactly how the pruning process occurs and what factors influence the selection of synapses to be pruned, it is still highly likely that educational experiences during this period do affect this process. Educators often notice a narrowing of children's interests and a greater focus on specific skills (e.g., a sport, a hobby), as well as an abandonment of effort in other areas (e.g., math, singing). They should probably discourage the tendency for children ages 8 to 14 to decide prematurely that certain content areas are "not their thing." For example, intense focus on a particular sport (e.g., soccer) to the exclusion of other activities may or may not be beneficial as synaptic pruning begins in earnest. It is unclear whether this focusing is inevitable as pruning occurs or whether encouragement of broad skills, as well as greater mastery of a few

skills, will result in a more efficient brain organization. At the least, educators can be cognizant of how their support or lack of support for skill development in specific content areas may affect brain organization during this age period.

2)   Although little research links formal operational thought processes (which become evident at the latter part of this age period) to brain structure/function development, parallels in the psychological and neurobiological realms can be hypothesized. As with the developmental milestones of earlier ages, educators can assume that the pruning, which results in faster and more efficient thought processes, also may be reflected in children's ability to think abstractly and hypothetically. Therefore, development of metacognitive and memory strategies is likely to be a good educational goal. Such strategies help children in this age period to "wire-in" synaptic connections in frontal lobe areas more specifically.

3)   Educator attention to the possible effects of gender specialization, which often occurs at this age, is also of interest. Although male and female adult brains seem to show some differences (albeit with a wide overlap between genders), relatively few differences are seen in young girls' and boys' brain structure and function. During this age period, the narrowing of interests in some areas and focusing of interests in others often occur differentially for girls and boys. For example, although a body of research shows that boys and girls perform equally well on mathematics in 4th grade (e.g., Fennema & Sherman, 1977), many girls seem to abandon mathematical interests during this age period. Similarly, boys who continue to have interests in music and dance or other artistic areas may be ostracized by other boys, and this peer pressure may cause boys to narrow their content interests. Until specifics of the interaction of genetic and environmental factors on brain pruning are better known, educators should probably encourage nonstereotypic and wide, rather than narrow, specialization of interests and experiences for both boys and girls during this age period.

4)   Educators should implement a number of responses for children who have had TBI. First, they must be alert to its effects on current skills. For example, children may have fatigue or reduced stamina following TBI, which may be partially due to medication, prolonged hospitalization, and inactivity. Daily activities may require more concentration from such children, because of cognitive and motor weaknesses, leading to higher levels of fatigue. Educators must be sure they do not confuse fatigue, stamina, and learning difficulties with motivation deficits or "laziness." Although these children may score at grade level on an achievement test after TBI, this score does not accurately reflect current functioning because such performances usually require use of overlearned skills. Even if the children score well, they may not be ready to return to regular education, because they may have difficulty with new learning. Special education services will be critical to address these children's needs.

Of course, the best intervention for TBI is prevention. Injury prevention includes both training for families and educators in supervisory practices; modifications of the home, educare, and school environments; and use of accident prevention strategies. For example, safety seats should be used by preschoolers and bicycle helmets by children who are riding bicycles, skateboarding, or engaging in similar activities. Safety education programs alone are often ineffective, however, and should be combined with legislation and appropriate environmental support if they are to be most successful (Tremblay & Peterson, 1999). Generally speaking, children with TBI should avoid contact sports, diving, or other activities involving a risk for a blow to the head. When such children return to school, they will need increased supervision and modifications of physical environments (e.g., hallway travel practices) to promote safety. Educators should be aware that TBI children's deficits in judgment and reasoning place them at risk for dangerous behaviors, even within the presumably "safe" school environment.

CHAPTER 6

Evaluating Childhood Education Practices in the Light of Present and Future Brain Research

When beginning work on this book, the authors initially intended to clarify for educators how the knowledge that has been derived from research on brain growth and neurological development could support or offer suggestions for present educational practice. As the preceding chapters make evident, this research is only beginning to address questions of how genetics and environment interact to influence brain development; the research is certainly not at a stage that can offer definitive information about the effects of specific educational practices on such development. Thus, the only way that the authors' goal can be addressed is through hypothesis generation, with the hope that educators and neuroscientists will join forces to test these hypotheses. Therefore, two types of hypotheses will be discussed: implications for specific educational practices and implications for advocacy of high-quality childhood education environments.

Implications of Brain Research for Specific Educational Practices

Most educators support many basic principles of childhood education. The effectiveness of some may be partially explained through inferences from present research-based knowledge of brain growth and neurological development. This review will hypothesize about the brain development-education relationships that may underlie some of these principles. It is the authors' intent only to speculate and to engage the reader in critical thinking about these relationships, not to make definitive statements. Many areas would be fertile ground for further brain-education research.

Art and Music Early Experiences

In spite of recent popular media attention to the potential positive effects of early exposure to art and music on brain growth and neurological development (e.g., music enhances spatial skills), no studies have examined such effects over short time periods or longitudinally. Nevertheless, some policymakers are promoting the playing of classical music to infants (*Omaha World Herald*, 1999). Anyone who has been around young children knows that they have high motivation to attend to and explore visual arts media and the rhythms, melodies, and tempos of music. Indeed, during the first years, children develop these abilities concurrently with language expression and motor coordination abilities. How these synaptic connections are formed is poorly understood at present; studies of adult brain functioning during visual art and auditory musical experiences, however, show that experience is related to variations in how fully such adult brain areas are engaged (Elbert et al., 1995). It seems likely that educational experiences with art and music can enhance synaptogenesis greatly in certain brain structures, and the pruning process may explain why some persons continue to refine their skills in artistic areas, while others rarely use such skills. From the standpoint of educational practice, giving children many opportunities to have visual art and music experiences probably promotes the development of the neurological networks that are related to such activities and increases the likelihood that children will become adept in such expression. Until longitudinal research more fully addresses these questions, however, early exposure to specific art and music experiences (e.g., Mozart) does not "guarantee" that children will be more adept at any particular skills (e.g., spatial awareness).

Computers and Other "Smart" Toys

Although some studies highlight the positive social interactions that occur during computer use and some evidence indicates that metacognition may be enhanced with programming experiences (Clements & Sarama, 1997; Evard, 1996; Miller, Church, & Trexler, 2000), the effects of computer use on brain growth and neurological development over time have not been documented. Even less is known about the effects of "smart" toys, which have computer chips that make the toys act and "speak" in ways that stimulate reactions from children (Bergen, 2001). Informal observations and narrative accounts of children who have used computers extensively suggest that cognitive "multi-tasking" may be enhanced and social skills may develop in different ways (e.g., electronic "friends" supplant face-to-face ones). In the absence of some longitudinal study, whether such behavioral changes are reflected in brain structures or neurological functions is not yet known.

From the standpoint of educational practice, educators would probably do best to encourage information gathering from a range of sources (e.g., reading, discussions, authentic experiences), rather than primarily from computer-generated sources. Similarly, children need real friends as well as virtual friends. As the pruning process begins to pick up speed in middle childhood, some children seem to become more and more engrossed in electronic information media. Brain research is vitally needed to determine whether the brains of children who use these media extensively may be developing somewhat differently. Whether a "technological brain" is adaptive for contemporary culture and should be encouraged is a matter of debate. Until data are available concerning what brain structure and neurological development differences might be fostered in computer-enhanced environments, educators will probably wish to take the middle road by encouraging technology-based activities without the loss of other means of knowledge construction.

Cooperative Learning

The cooperative learning literature (e.g., Johnson & Johnson, 1994; Slavin, 1995) makes a strong case for the efficacy of social-emotional factors in enhancing cognition and academic skill development. Research on cooperative learning offers evidence that cognition can develop well within a supportive social-emotional environment, especially in cooperative learning groups. It also provides many suggestions for enhancing the effectiveness of such cooperative learning. Hypothetically, this educational practice can be supported by the evidence from brain research that emotion and cognition are more closely tied than previously thought and that the ability to form social attachments may be traced to certain brain structures and functions. To date, no research has examined how cooperative social interactions may affect brain structural growth or neurological development, although research is beginning to link possible brain anomalies to problems in social-emotional and cognitive functioning (e.g., in autism and ADHD). In line with other suggestions for educational practice, providing cooperative learning experiences that may stimulate synaptogenesis in the brain's social-emotional networks may be a useful practice. However, other types of learning experiences are also important.

Critical Periods for Timing Certain Educational Experiences

After neuroimaging research described the rapid occurrence of synaptogenesis in infancy, researchers speculated that there may be brief critical periods during which certain aspects of brain growth and neurological development must occur. They hypothesized that certain specific environmental interventions (e.g., hearing classical music, teaching sound/symbol correspondence) could be especially influential during such critical periods. There do seem to be a few brief critical periods in prenatal brain growth and neurological development (e.g., cortical migration), and some areas of the brain (e.g, the visual cortex) have relatively short periods (age 1-2) of synaptic overproduction, with synaptic pruning then beginning by ages 3-5. Nevertheless, researchers debate about whether the terminology "critical periods" should be used.

Most researchers and educators are now using the term "sensitive periods" to suggest that while specific aspects of brain growth and neurological development appear at particular time periods, these time periods are long rather than brief. For example, the optimal period for development of emotional attachment seems to be during the first year, and language development seems to be a focus during the first 2 to 3 years. However, humans do not "bond" emotionally in a brief critical period right after birth, but rather seem to have a sensitive period during the first year in which such emotional attachments develop; they can form attachments after this period as well. Receptive language seems to have a shorter sensitive period (beginning in the latter part of the first year) than does language expression, which can occur over a wide time period—at least through the early childhood years. Motor development also seems to follow a sensitive, but not a critical, time schedule. Certain skills, such as absolute pitch in music, also seem to be lost by late childhood if not exercised earlier. The types of experiences provided during the years from birth to 14 certainly will affect brain growth and neurological development, but a concentrated effort to impart certain content during particularly identified brief periods is not necessarily warranted. The brain's plasticity makes the theory of short critical periods for brain growth and neurological development unlikely. For educators, this means that they should not "give up" on any child just because that child did not have certain experiences during an optimum sensitive time period. Although the young brain has more plasticity, the brain's ability to make structural and functional changes when encountering new experiences is evident throughout the lifespan. (For an in-depth look at the issues surrounding the critical periods debate, see Bailey, Bruer, Symons, & Lichtman, 2001.)

Developmentally Appropriate Practice (DAP)

The early childhood field in particular has stressed the need for developmentally appropriate experiences; that is, experiences should be designed to fit children's typical patterns of cognitive, motor, sensory, social-emotional, and language development. This belief sometimes results in educators' hesitancy to teach skills that are not primarily generated by children's own exploration of their environment. In general, the presently available information from brain research would be compatible with DAP. The amazing plasticity of the brain and the phenomenal growth in synapses during the early years would also suggest that, with adult scaffolding, young children may be capable of learning information and skills that have not been traditional parts of the early childhood curriculum. Nevertheless, educators should not be buying vigorously marketed "brain-based curricula," as most of it has no basis in brain research. Educators can, however, strive to expand children's experiences in developmentally appropriate ways in order to facilitate synaptogenesis. For example, the DAP guidelines regarding active learning and the availability of a wide choice of experiences seem to be in line with present knowledge of brain growth and neurological development.

Emotional Development As an Educational Goal

Brain research is bringing about some changes to the simplistic "triune" brain model, which hypothesized that emotions were centered in the "mammalian" brain (i.e., the limbic system). It is now known that strong interactive linkages exist between the structures that generate emotions and the structures that recognize and control emotions, which are primarily in the "neomammalian" brain (i.e., the cerebral cortex). Although infants show and recognize most emotions, as children's brains mature, they gain the capacity to label, categorize, and interpret emotions. These processes in turn affect what basic emotions children experience and what cognitive, language, and social meanings they retain. Research on episodic memory also indicates that the best remembered events are those embedded in strong emotions (both positive and negative). Educators can use this knowledge by being aware of the emotional aspects of learning and trying to enhance the learning of important content by providing experiences that are embedded in positive emotional contexts. Although no imaging studies of brain activation during emotion-based learning experiences have been done, it is likely that brain research would support educator awareness of how emotions can "wire-in" some indelible learnings. Most people can recall a school experience with either a positive or negative emotional tone that permanently affected their learning of some content area!

Fine/Gross Motor Development As an Educational Goal

Brain areas involved in motor and sensory activities have been studied quite extensively, and one of the most interesting findings is that actions that require precise movement and motor coordination take up more space in the motor cortex than do broader but less demanding activities. For example, the motor cortex allots more space to actions of the tongue and lips than to the foot. Educators have always known that children require much motor action, both for its own sake and for its ability to strengthen the learning of other information. Thus, especially when teaching younger children, educators include motor action with many learning activities. Learning to inhibit motor activity is also important, especially for development of certain areas of the brain; the complexity of the interactions among various brain areas that are required to inhibit or to coordinate actions is still being explored. As a general rule, allowing children to have multisensory input and to be motorically active while learning is important. However, emphasizing specific movements (e.g., crawling) or movement routines (e.g., exercising the right hemisphere by certain left-side body movements) is not as yet supported by brain research. Being required to sit for long hours without opportunity to engage in motor actions should certainly not be a common practice in schools. Educators may be able to support "learning by doing" as congruent with brain research.

First and Second Language Learning

Many educators and parents express interest in providing second language experiences during the time period when a first language typically is acquired. Research shows that when more than one language is learned in early childhood, both languages are housed in the same section (the left hemisphere) of the brain; when a second language is learned later in life, additional brain sections (a bilateral site) are used for the second language (Weber-Fox & Neville, 1996). Some research also shows that discrimination and reproduction of non-native-language phonemes diminishes with age (Bortfield & Whitehurst, 2000). Thus, evidence exists that second (or third) language learning should be initiated before—or at least by—middle childhood. While such language learning appears to be facilitated at those ages, the ability to learn another language remains throughout life; the brain's plasticity allows adaptations to accommodate a new language. Because the ability to recognize and reproduce sounds of the non-native language diminishes with age, however, foreign language speakers who learn at later ages typically have a recognizable accent. In regard to educational practice, it does seem that the optimum time for teaching a second language may be earlier than middle school or high school, when foreign language classes traditionally are taught in the United States.

Health and Nutrition Education

Evidence from prenatal and infancy brain research clearly indicates the importance of adequate nutrition and good health practices (e.g., avoiding drug use) during that time period. Because brain growth (size and weight) is essentially over by early childhood, and because the brain uses such a large proportion of body energy, the brain is especially vulnerable to the effects of poor nutrition, teratogenic substances, or disease. Educators can work with parents to help them enhance the nutrition and health of their children (including prenatally), and work with students to stress the importance of lifelong nutrition and health. They can inform children about the nutritional content of "fast" foods and link good brain nourishment to good thinking practices. As of this time, clear research-based evidence that particular "brain foods" can enhance brain growth and development does not exist.

Inclusion

One of the major rationales for inclusion of children with disabilities into classrooms with other children is that they will gain more relevant social experiences and cognitive stimulation than they will receive in separate "resource room" programs. While brain research does not speak directly to this issue, some inferences might be drawn on both sides of the inclusion debate. On the side of inclusion is the argument that exposure to a wide range of experiences, such as found in a regular classroom, and being challenged at their highest levels of ability might enhance brain growth and neurological development in children with disabilities by increasing the variety and richness of their synapses. On the other hand, being in a classroom with only a few other children and an educator who can provide intensive experiences in a smaller number of areas also might strengthen essential synaptic connections in functional areas, thus helping these children develop competent skills for operating in the larger society. Studying the brain structures and functions of children with learning disabilities, autistic spectrum disorder, and attention deficit hyperactivity disorder may shed further light on this debate in the future. Some major findings may help resolve the question of what type of educational setting is best for children with specific types of disabilities.

Intervention Practices

The specific intervention practices that are most effective with children with various disabilities also are subject to debate, and proponents of one approach (e.g., ABA; Lovaas & Smith, 1988) often see little of value in other approaches (e.g., TEACCH; Schopler, 1996). One practical result of early intervention has been that rich early experiences, of whatever type, seem to have benefited many children (Campbell & Ramey, 1994). Although special educators, physical and occupational therapists, and other professionals working with children who have disabilities promote many specific intervention practices (e.g., sensory integration), brain research has not yet uncovered evidence to support one intervention approach over another, despite proponents' claims about neurological benefits. As with inclusion, research now being conducted may result in more definitive answers regarding interventions. Although details of how such interventions specifically affect brain structures and functions are sparse, certain interventions clearly have a positive effect on some children. Definitive studies with large samples that connect intervention practices to brain development need to be done.

Left Brain/Right Brain Teaching Strategies

While brain research delineates some differences in the structures and functions of the two brain hemispheres and in the corpus callosum, recommendations about teaching to the left brain or right brain far exceed the research evidence. This approach is especially problematic when linked to gender differences, especially if it results in differentiated educational opportunities for boys and girls. From an educational practice perspective, experiences that strengthen all areas of the brain for all children are probably most effective. One value of this research is educators' increased awareness that educational experiences should not be solely of a language/logic nature. By broadening experiences to include those that purportedly are more closely allied to the "right brain" (e.g., the arts, social-emotional, spatial), educators can enhance the overall curriculum. Because the brain is an integrated entity, however, educators should not encourage children to think of themselves as either "right-brained" or "left-brained." They should help children build skills in all areas.

Memory Teaching Strategies

Memory is one of the most intriguing areas being studied in psychological research. Researchers offer numerous theories to explain memory, and they describe various types of memory using computer-like and other models (e.g., short term, long term, working, procedural, episodic). What they never have discovered, however, is just exactly what memory is and where it resides in the brain. Some clues about memory can be found in brain research findings, and most of these clues point to a number of brain structures being involved in memory; some evidence suggests that neurological connections hold memory as well. From an education standpoint, one of the most useful findings of brain research may be that many parts of the brain are involved in memory. Thus, helping children learn memory strategies that call upon varied functions of the brain (e.g., visual, auditory, motor, emotional) can enhance their memory capabilities and strengthen synaptic connections for learning. It is likely that the more memory links that can be "hard-wired" into the brain before synaptic pruning begins, the greater memory abilities in general will be. Brain research holds the key to unlocking the mystery of memory.

Metacognitive Teaching Strategies

An even greater mystery is that of metacognition, which is the ability to think about one's own thinking. Metacognition is one aspect of "consciousness," and brain research currently offers few answers as to how or where it occurs. Research on the frontal lobe does identify this site as being involved in a number of thinking processes that are related to metacognition, such as predicting, analyzing, and evaluating experiences. Research on brains (especially the frontal lobes) of individuals who seem to lack these skills may provide answers to the question of metacognition. Even if the precise site of metacognitive strategies in the brain is unclear, it is especially important for educators to facilitate children's development of metacognitive strategies, because they provide the basis for formal operations and other abstract thought. With older students, Cardellichio and Field (1997) make a case for efforts to "overcome the brain's natural tendency to limit information" by using teaching strategies that provoke divergent and hypothetical thinking, application of different symbol systems, and use of analogy and web analysis. The true mystery of the processes of metacognition will not be solved until brain researchers understand what is involved in consciousness.

Multiple Intelligences Teaching Strategies

Howard Gardner's multiple intelligences theory is very popular in educational circles, and a number of curricula purport to be based on the tenets of his theory. Some provide a wide range of classroom activities in order to "exercise all" intelligences, while others focus on teaching to children's supposed intellectual strengths and weaknesses (i.e., their "learning styles"). While some evidence indicates that certain parts of the brain are more active during particular types of learning experiences (e.g., visual and language areas active in reading), no studies show one-to-one correspondences between parts of the brain and the particular intelligences supposedly being exercised during teaching activities. Gardner expresses concern that interpretations of his theory sometimes result in teaching for specific "learning styles" based on the intelligence dimensions he outlined (Checkley, 1997). Until more is known about the neurological bases for multiple intelligence theory, the best strategy for educators is probably one of giving children opportunities to engage all modes of intelligence and to gain mastery of as many as possible.

New Math and Old Math

Although proponents of some "brain-based" curricula stress that such curricula help children learn mathematical concepts more effectively, applying brain research to the teaching of mathematics presently relies on a number of unsupported assumptions. Certain aspects of mathematics involve the use of spatial skills, while others are primarily related to symbol understanding and use of algorithms. Manipulating mathematical quantities with concrete objects is vastly different from manipulations with symbol systems. Learning the ordering of geometric patterns of shapes/sizes probably involves different areas of the brain than memorizing the multiplication tables. Recent "new" math emphasis on critical thinking and problem-solving skills may enhance frontal lobe development, while "old" math attention to learning algorithms and number facts may further development of brain areas that are activated by memory tasks. It is probably the case that giving children exposure to both new and old math methods may give the greatest stimulation to the brain. At present, no developmental research links brain growth and neurological development to specific mathematical teaching methods.

Oral Language and Emerging Literacy

A body of research evidence supports the view that the earliest years of life (ages 1 to 4) are the optimum time for extensive development of oral language, especially in regard to phonological and syntactical rule learning. For language expression, the "range of normality" is quite wide, however. Vocabulary also increases greatly, although it will continue to develop throughout life. Research also indicates that emerging literacy skills begin to develop in infancy, especially when parents interact in book "reading" early on. Thus, there appears to be a sensitive period in which such skills develop more easily, and evidence points to a genetic/environment interaction that promotes such development. However, no brain research findings support urging the specific teaching of literacy skills (such as phonics) in infancy in order to further precocity. That is, no evidence exists that direct teaching of language/literacy at early ages has a significant effect on brain growth and neurological development. Much emphasis is being put on strategies to teach emerging literacy during the 3 to 5 age period; some academic research suggests this type of literacy understanding is essential for later reading excellence. Educators can rely on the psychological and educational research to support their efforts to foster emerging literacy, without resorting to the limited research linking certain brain areas to literacy development.

Play in the Curriculum

As proponents of play, most early childhood educators would argue that play provides the wide range of stimulating experiences that would likely foster synaptogenesis. Research shows that play enhances cognitive, social-emotional, and motor skills. The importance of play has not been related to brain research except in a few instances, such as in Panksepp's (1998) speculations, drawn from studies of ADHD, that play may aid maturation of the frontal cortex. Play does serve a number of important functions that can be hypothetically related to brain research. For example, play is highly motivating to young children and they are inclined to repeat enjoyable activities in play. The repetition and elaboration of "practice play" may strengthen synaptic connections and create levels of mastery that contribute to brain growth and neurological development. Pretend play has long been related to the exercise of some brain functions, such as symbolic representation, imagination, social-emotional control, and language use. Game playing often involves qualities of both practice and pretend play, and also fosters skills of prediction, self-regulation, and motor coordination. As Sylwester noted (1995), the frontal lobe's "extra" capacity, useful for problem solving in emergencies, can be exercised in non-emergency times by creating problems to solve in imaginary and playful realms. Thus, while research evidence linking play development to specific areas of neurological development is lacking, educators who give opportunities for play are likely to be supporting brain functioning.

Pro-social and Social Skill Development As Educational Goals

One goal of education is to help children develop pro-social styles of interaction that will increase their social skills over time. Much psychological research using behavioral observation has been devoted to this area of development, resulting in a body of literature on social skills training (e.g., Topping, Holmes, & Brenner, 2000). This work has not as yet been connected to brain research. Problems with social interaction have been noted in children who have had brain trauma, autism, and other disabilities. For example, rehabilitation psychologists studying pro-social and anti-social behaviors in children with brain trauma found interventions that focused on specific skills retraining in "real world" situations to be most efficacious. Individuals with brain damage recover trained skills more quickly and consistently than they recover spontaneous, appropriate, social, and adaptive behaviors (Park & Ingles, 2000). Children from abusive or neglectful environments also may have poor social skills. Early adolescent bullying and other anti-social actions are other evidences of poor social skills development. Promising research is underway that may give clues to educators about whether such behaviors are linked to anomalies in brain development. At this point, educators can be aware that children who have been in abusive or neglectful environments, have experienced traumatic brain injury, or have a disability may need special help in learning prosocial skills.

Self-Esteem and Self-Efficacy

An extensive body of research covers aspects of self-concept development, especially in relation to self-esteem (i.e., having a global evaluative sense of self). More recently, researchers are examining the concept of self-efficacy (i.e., having a sense of agency regarding one's ability to achieve specific goals) (Bandura, 1997). Most research on the "self" is theoretically based and relies primarily on observational and self-report data. Some evidence suggests, however, that serotonin levels in the brain differ in individuals with high and low self-esteem, with high serotonin levels related to high self-esteem (Sylwester, 1995). It is presently unclear whether areas in the brain are activated differentially when success or failure follows an effort or when an individual perceives the approval or disapproval of others. One hypothesis is that children may feel more effective and may receive more positive feedback from others as neural pathways become strengthened or expanded in developmentally appropriate ways. At this point, however, the debate about which comes first—getting positive feedback that then results in efficacy feelings or having successful experiences that then affect one's global sense of self—cannot be answered by brain research. Efforts to support these areas of development certainly are warranted, but how brain structures or functions relate to these experiences is in need of study.

Standards-based Education/Curriculum Alignment

Because evidence suggests that schooling affects brain growth and neurological development, the current emphasis on standards-based education and curriculum alignment with state proficiency tests is likely to have an impact on brain development, especially at the ages when pruning begins in earnest. Ways of thinking that help children perform well on such tests may be strengthened as pruning occurs, and test-taking skills that are practiced in schools may remain with individuals across the lifespan. Educators may worry that excessive focus on learning the standards-based information and being tested frequently on proficiency tests may change brains negatively in some way; at present, there is no evidence to suggest positive or negative effects. No one has conducted a longitudinal study of brain changes as a result of school practices such as curriculum alignment with tests. It seems likely that memory pathways would be affected by the educational focus of the curriculum, and these effects may be positive in some ways and negative in others. For example, if educators promote "overlearning" of certain content areas crucial to the tests (e.g., reading, math), this is likely to strengthen those neuronal circuits and prune some others. Or if educators stress metacognitive activities designed to aid problem solving and making inferences (if these are to be tested), those areas of the brain might be strengthened. Effects on children's brains will depend on how educators "teach to the test," because whatever is emphasized in learning will influence brain development.

Whole Language/Phonics Training

Although debates over the extremes of whole language and phonics still rage in some quarters, and some very poor examples of extreme practices do exist on each end of the spectrum, most educators acknowledge that both approaches are useful for helping most children learn to read. Brain research with individuals suffering from learning disabilities provides a few clues that might guide educational practice. However, these studies are still at a early stage. Research on the general structures and functions of the brain suggests that children must have both the ability to put together the specifics of sound/symbol correspondence (bottom-up approach) and the meaning-making strategies promoted by whole language (top-down approach), although these two abilities may be sited in different areas of the brain. Because the brain operates as an integrated whole, children become readers once they can put all the skills needed for reading together. The educator's role is thus partly to serve as a "detective" when children have difficulty making sense of either phonics or whole language instruction. Upon identifying the missing skills, the educator then provides scaffolding to encourage development of those skills. At present, only minimal evidence indicates that language/literacy training affects brain structures, but the direction of that evidence is toward increases in the areas of the brain concerned with literacy. It is likely, therefore, that these different methods would result in different development within the brain.

IMPLICATIONS OF BRAIN RESEARCH FOR ADVOCACY OF EXCELLENCE IN CHILDHOOD EDUCATION

While brain research does not address specific educational practices, it does offer some clear direction on a number of advocacy issues that should be of concern for educators. The major issues, briefly discussed here, are prenatal care, safe environments, quality early child care and education, and knowledgeable educators.

Excellence of Prenatal Care

Excellent prenatal care is clearly important to brain growth and neurological development. The lack of such care is a global problem that all interested parties must address in cooperation, including parents and parents-to-be, educators, medical personnel, state and local government officials, and other concerned citizens. This is one topic on which the brain research implications are clear, and it is tragic that many still consider early and effective prenatal care as an option rather than a necessity. Educators can strive to have the best impact in two ways: 1) working with parents and children in Early Start and other home visit programs, and in Head Start and other preschool programs, to bring about knowledge dissemination and change; and 2) communicating with legislators and supporting worldwide organizations that provide information about the importance of prenatal care and generate funding to help women obtain it.

Safe Environments

Safe environments include conditions of both physical and social-emotional safety. Concerns related to school physical facilities and safety practices should, of course, be addressed; too many substandard buildings in unsafe environments are serving as education sites. Furthermore, many children do not feel safe in the school environ-ment. Most researchers on brain development would agree that social-emotional safety during the first years of a child's life is essential for healthy brain growth and neuro-logical development; such feelings of security also contribute to sustained optimum brain development throughout childhood. Many children throughout the world, in-cluding the United States, do not have such environments. Furthermore, many chil-dren are subject to child abuse and neglect, despite efforts to prevent such conditions. Educators often see children at school who are hypervigilant, fearful, and/or unable to concentrate on learning. In cases where abuse or neglect contributes to such learning problems, it is likely that brain growth and neurological development are being af-fected negatively. This is another area that warrants more brain research to clarify which factors in a set of related conditions are primary. The resulting evidence must lead the way in promoting safe environments for all children throughout the world. Perhaps as the messages from brain research gain a wider audience, the impetus for providing both physically and social-emotionally safe environments will be strengthened. Educators can work with groups who are concerned about these issues, and strive to provide children with a sense of safety in their school or preschool environments.

Quality Early Child Care and Education

Brain research findings offer some general support to calls for high-quality early child care and education programs. Research on child care shows that consistency of educarers and educators aids early attachment development, and that high-quality programs fa-cilitate cognitive and social development (National Institutes of Child Health and Hu-man Development [NICHD], 1999). While the exact nature of the links between brain growth and neurological development and high-quality care and education have not been studied, the clear importance of the early years in terms of brain development reinforces the need for all children to have good early learning experiences. Recently, NICHD researchers reported longitudinal results that show not only relationships be-tween high-quality care and positive language and intellectual development, but also some relationships between negative behaviors and long periods of time spent in child care; however, this study did not monitor effects on brain growth and neurological development (NICHD, 2001). Advocates for high-quality programs draw upon the brain research literature to strengthen their recommendations and emphasize the im-portance of brain development in early childhood (Shonkoff & Phillips, 2000). Pres-ently available research, however, does not address the specific connections of early care and education to optimum brain development. As these authors emphasize,

Developmental neuroscience research says a great deal about the conditions that pose dangers to the developing brain and from which young children need to be protected. It says virtually nothing about what to do to create enhanced or accelerated brain development. (p. 183)

Knowledgeable Educators

Research also shows that educators who have a good knowledge of children's develop-mental needs and of methods for facilitating their development do have more success in enhancing child growth and development (Bowman, Donovan, & Burns, 2000). While brain researchers have not specifically evaluated brain growth and neurological development in relation to educators' educational levels, psychological and educational researchers have documented this often. Future research should explore just what aspects of an educated person's behavior most strongly interact with children's brain growth and neurological development. Current research efforts are investigating characteristics of knowledgeable educarers and educators in quality programs and relating them to cognitive, language, and social-emotional development (NICHD, 2001); however, these studies do not specifically link educator training and behavior to children's brain growth and neurological development. Research on educator knowledge and behavior does provide insights into models of interaction that could be emulated by parents, educarers, and educators who do not have high levels of formal education.

Summary

Although available research offers much information about the brain and the processes involved in its growth and neurological development, this information barely scratches the surface in terms of implications for education. While many current educational practices likely have some effect on brain structures and functions, none of these practices are validated by current brain research. Until such time that definitive research-based information is available, it is important that educators evaluate the emerging research carefully and reject exaggerated claims asserting that a particular "brain-based" curriculum must be adopted. Caine and Caine (1991, pp. 29-30) offer some general implications of brain research for education: 1) the beginning of life is critical, 2) learning and maturation cannot be separated, 3) the environment affects the brain physiologically, and 4) the time scale of change varies enormously among children.

Because brain research findings do demonstrate potentially lasting negative effects on the brain as a result of extremely poor environmental conditions, educators should be in the forefront of advocacy for the improvement of such environmental conditions so that children are not at risk for those negative effects. Thompson and Nelson (2001) state that

Enhanced public information about the importance of prenatal care, early nutrition, immunizations, and elimination of environmental toxins may accomplish as much to promote early brain development as public information campaigns focusing on the significance of talking and singing to young infants. (p. 12)

While they recognize the need for brain research to inform care and education, Thompson and Nelson say that "contrary to the impression created by some media accounts, researchers are at the vanguard—not the end—of exciting new discoveries about brain development" (p. 12), and they call for more linkages between what neuroscientists know and what educators know.

Lichtman (2001) points out that "given the ability of experience to alter the connections in the brains of children, educators are in essence brain engineers, applied scientists who could, in principle, use the available information as a means of informing their educational practice and policies" (p. 41). He laments that this "bridge between disciplines" is not yet in place because neuroscientists have not communicated their work in ways that allow "critical scrutiny" by educators, and because many higher learning processes are "out of reach of invasive research." He calls on educators to initiate communication with neuroscientists to give them more information about how the human brain learns.

While educators should resolve to stay current with new research findings, they also should continue to base their educational practices on their professional knowledge of development and learning processes. As Gopnik, Meltzoff, and Kuhl (1999) remind educators, "Understanding the mind helps us understand the brain as much as or more than understanding the brain helps us to understand the mind" (p. 175). Educators also should remember that the brain's plasticity makes learning a lifelong function of the brain. All educational practices that expand learning experiences and challenge thinking can be influences on brain growth and neurological development, because brains are in part "created" by each individual. This holds true throughout infancy, childhood, adolescence, and even into the adult years.

References

Abell, F., Krama, M., Ashburner, J., Passingham, R., Firston, K., Frackowiak, R., Happe, F., Frith, C., & Grith, U. (1999). The neuroanatomy of autism: A voxel-based whole brain analysis of structural scans. *Neuroreport, 10*(8), 1647-1651.

Allen, G., Buxton, R. B., Wong, E. C., & Courchesne, E. (1997). Attentional activation of the cerebellum independent of motor involvement. *Science, 275,* 1940-1943.

Bailey, D. B., Bruer, J. T., Symons, F. J., & Lichtman, J. W. (Eds.). (2001). *Critical thinking about critical periods.* Baltimore: Paul H. Brookes.

Bandura, A. (1997). *Self-efficacy: The exercise of control.* New York: W. H. Freeman.

Benasich, A. A., & Spitz, R. V. (1998). Insights from infants: Temporal processing abilities and genetics contribute to language development. In G. Willems & K. Whitmore (Eds.), *A neurodevelopmental approach to specific learning disorders* (pp. 191-210). London: MacKeith Press.

Benes, F. M., Turtle, M., Khan, Y., & Farol, P. (1994). Myelination of a key relay zone in the hippocampal formation occurs in the human brain during childhood, adolescence, and adulthood. *Archives of General Psychiatry, 51*(6), 477-484.

Bergen, D. (2001). Learning in the robotic world: Active or reactive? *Childhood Education, 77,* 249-250.

Bergen, D., Reid, R., & Torelli, L. (2001). *Educating and caring for very young children: The infant/toddler curriculum.* New York: Teachers College Press.

Bergen, D., Smith, K., & O'Neill, S. (1989). Designing play environments for infants and toddlers. In D. Bergen (Ed.), *Play as a medium for learning and development* (pp. 187-207). Portsmouth, NH: Heinemann.

Bortfield, H., & Whitehurst, G. J. (2000). Sensitive periods in first language acquisition. In D. B. Bailey, J. T. Bruer, F. J. Symons, & J. W. Lichtman (Eds.), *Critical thinking about critical periods* (pp. 173-190). Baltimore: Paul H. Brookes.

Bowman, B., Donovan, M. S., & Burns, M. S. (2000). *Eager to learn: Educating our preschoolers. Executive Summary, Committee on Early Childhood Pedagogy, Commission on Behavioral and Social Sciences and Education, National Research Council.* Washington, DC: National Academy Press.

Brash, S., Maranta, G., Murphy, W., & Walker, B. (1990). *How things work: The brain.* Alexandria, VA: Time-Life.

Bremner, J. D., Randall, P., Vermetten, E., Staib, L., et al. (1997). Magnetic resonance imaging-based measurement of hippocampal volume in posttraumatic stress disorder related to childhood physical and sexual abuse: A preliminary report. *Biological Psychiatry, 41*(1), 23-32.

Bruer, J. T. (1999). In search of . . . brain-based education. *Phi Delta Kappan, 80,* 649-657.

Caine, R. N., & Caine, G. (1991). *Making connections: Teaching and the human brain.* Alexandria, VA: Association for Supervision and Curriculum Development.

Campbell, F. A., & Ramey, C. T. (1994). Effects of early intervention on intellectual and academic achievement: A follow-up study of children from low-income families. *Child Development, 65,* 684-698.

Cardellichio, T., & Field, W. (1997). Seven strategies that encourage neural branching. *Educational Leadership, 54*(6), 33-36.

Carlson, M., & Earls, F. (1997). Psychological and neuroendocrinological sequelae of early social deprivation in institutionalized children in Romania. In C. S. Carter, I. I. Lederhendler, & B. Kirkpatrick (Eds.), *The integrative neurobiology of affiliation* (pp. 419-428). New York: New York Academy of Sciences.

Carper, R. A., & Courchesne, E. (2000). Inverse correlation between frontal lobe and cerebellum sizes in children with autism. *Brain, 123*, 836-844.

Checkley, K. (1997). The first seven . . . and the eighth: A conversation with Howard Gardner. *Educational Leadership, 55*(1), 8-13.

Chiron, C., Jambaque, I., Nabbout, R., Lounes, R., Syrota, A., & Dulac, O. (1997). The right brain hemisphere is dominant in human infants. *Brain, 120*(6), 1057-1065.

Chugani, H. T. (1999). PET scanning studies of human brain development and plasticity. *Developmental Neuropsychology, 16*(3), 379-381.

Chugani, H. T., Phelps, M. E., & Mazziotta, J. C. (1993). Positron emission tomography study of human brain functional development. In M. H. Johnson (Ed.), *Brain development and cognition: A reader* (pp. 125-143). Oxford, England: Blackwell Publishers.

Clements, D. H., & Sarama, J. (1997). Research on Logo: A decade of progress. In C. D. Maddux & D. L. Johnson (Eds.), *Logo: A retrospective* (pp. 9-46). New York: Haworth Press.

Cohen, M., & Bookheimer, S. (1994). Localization of brain function using magnetic resonance imaging. *Trends in Neurosciences, 17*, 268-277.

Connolly, K., Brown, K., & Bassett, E. (1968). Developmental changes in some components of a motor skill. *British Journal of Psychology, 59*, 305-314.

CQO Study Team. (1995). *Cost, quality, & child outcomes in child care centers, technical report.* Denver, CO: University of Colorado at Denver.

Crick, F. (1994). *The astonishing hypothesis: The scientific search for the soul.* New York: Scribner.

Cytowic, R. E. (1993). *The man who tasted shapes.* New York: Putnam.

Dawson, G., Hessl, D., & Frey, K. (1994). Social influences on early developing biological and behavioral systems related to risk for affective disorder. *Development and Psychopathology, 6*(4), 759-779.

Dawson, G., Klinger, L., Panagiotides, H., Hill, D., & Spieker, S. (1992). Frontal lobe activity and affective behavior of infants of mothers with depressive symptoms. *Child Development, 63*, 725-737.

Dawson, G., Meltzoff, A. N., Osterling, J., & Rinaldi, J. (1998). Neuropsychological correlates of early symptoms of autism. *Child Development, 69*(5), 1276-1285.

DeBellis, M. D., Keshaven, M. S., Clark, D. B., Casey, B. J., Giedd, J. B., Boring, A. M., Frustaci, K., & Ryan, N. D. (1999). Developmental traumatology, Part 2: Brain development. *Biological Psychiatry, 45*, 1271-1284.

Denckla, M. B. (1974). Development of motor co-ordination in normal children. *Developmental Medical Child Neurology, 16*, 729-741.

Diamond, A., & Goldman-Rakic, P. S. (1989). Comparison of human infants and rhesus monkeys on Piaget's AB task: Evidence for dependence on dorsolateral prefrontal cortex. *Experimental Brain Research, 74*, 24-40.

Edelman, G. M. (1992). *Bright air, brilliant fire: On the matter of the mind.* New York: Basic Books.

Eden, G. F., Van Meter, J. W., Rumsey, J. M., Maisog, J. M., Woods, R. P., & Zeffiro, T. A. (1996). Abnormal processing of visual motion in dyslexia as revealed by functional brain imaging. *Nature, 382,* 66-69.

Elbert, T., Pantev, C., Wienbruch, C., Rockstroh, B., & Taub, E. (1995). Increased cortical representation of the fingers of the left hand in string players. *Science, 270,* 305-307.

Eliot, L. (1999). *What's going on in there? How the brain and mind develop in the first five years of life.* New York: Bantam.

Epstein, H. (1978). Growth spurts during brain development: Implications for educational policy and practice. In J. Chall & A. Mirsky (Eds.), *Education and the brain: 77th National Society for the Study of Education yearbook.* Chicago: Chicago University Press.

Evard, M. (1996). A community of designers. In Y. Kafai & M. Resnick (Eds.), *Constructionism in practice* (pp. 223-239). Mahwah, NJ: Erlbaum.

Faraone, S. V., & Biederman, J. (1998). Neurobiology of attention-deficit hyperactivity disorder. *Biological Psychiatry, 44*(10), 951-958.

Fennema, E., & Sherman, J. (1977). Sex-related differences in math achievement, spatial visualization, and affective factors. *American Educational Research Journal, 14,* 51-71.

Fiez, J. (1996). Cerebellar contributions to cognition. *Neuron, 16*(Jan), 13-15.

Finger, S. (1994). *Origins of neuroscience: A history of explorations into brain function.* New York: Oxford University Press.

Fischer, K. W., & Rose, S. P. (1998). Growth cycles of brain and mind. *Educational Leadership, 56*(3), 56-60.

Fletcher, J. M., Shaywitz, S. E., Shankweiler, D. P., Katz, L., Liberman, I. Y., Stuebing, K. K., Francis, D. J., Fowler, A. E., & Shaywitz, B. (1994). Cognitive profiles of reading disability: Comparisons of discrepancy and low achievement definitions. *Journal of Educational Psychology, 86*(1), 6-23.

Flowers, D. L., Wood, F. B., & Naylor, C. E. (1991). Regional cerebral blood flow correlates of language processes in reading disability. *Archives of Neurology, 48,* 637-643.

Fox, N. A., Rubin, K. H., Calkins, S. D., Marshall, T. R., Coplan, R. J., Porges, S. W., Long, J. M., & Stewart, S. (1995). Frontal activation asymmetry and social competence at four years of age. *Child Development, 66*(6), 1770-1784.

Fox, N. A., Schmidt, L. A., Calkins, S. D., & Rubin, K. H. (1996). The role of frontal activation in the regulation and dysregulation of social behavior during the preschool years. *Development & Psychopathology, 8*(1), 89-102.

Gibson, K. R. (1991). Myelination and behavioral development: A comparative perspective on questions of neoteny, altriciality, and intelligence. In K. R. Gibson & A. C. Petersen (Eds.), *Brain maturation and cognitive development: Comparative and cross-cultural perspectives* (pp. 29-63). New York: de Gruyter.

Giedd, J., Snell, J., Lange, N., Rajapakse, J., Casey, B., Kozuch, P., Vaituzis, A., Vauss, Y., Hamburger, S., Kaysen, D., & Rapoport, J. (1996). Quantitative magnetic resonance imaging of human brain development: Ages 4-18. *Cerebral Cortex, 6*(4), 551-560.

Gilkerson, L. (2001). Integrating an understanding of brain development into early childhood education. *Infant Mental Health Journal, 22*(1-2), 174-187.

Goldberg, S. (1990). *Clinical neuroanatomy made ridiculously simple.* Miami, FL: MedMaster, Inc.

Gopnik, A., Meltzoff, A. N., & Kuhl, P. K. (1999). *The scientist in the crib: What early learning tells us about the mind.* New York: HarperCollins.

Greenough, W. T., Cohen, N. J., & Juraska, J. M. (1999). New neurons in old brains: Learning to survive? *Nature Neuroscience, 2*(3), 203-205.

Greenspan, S. I., & Lewis, N. B. (1999). *Building healthy minds: The six experiences that create intelligence and emotional growth in babies and young children.* Cambridge, MA: Perseus.

Gross, C. G. (1998). *Brain, vision, memory: Tales in the history of neuroscience.* Cambridge, MA: MIT Press.

Hagman, J. O., Wood, F., Buchsbaum, M. S., Tallal, P., Flowers, L., & Katz, W. (1992). Cerebral brain metabolism in adult dyslexic subjects assessed with positron emission tomography during performance of an auditory task. *Archives of Neurology, 49,* 734-739.

Haier, J. (1993). Cerebral glucose metabolism and intelligence. In P. A. Vernon (Ed.), *Biological approaches to the study of human intelligence* (pp. 317-332). Norwood, NJ: Ablex.

Hale, S. (1990). A global developmental trend in cognitive processing speed. *Child Development, 61,* 653-663.

Hammer, C. S. (2001). "Come and sit down and let Mama read": Book reading interactions between African American mothers and their infants. In J. L. Harris & A. G. Kamhi (Eds.), *Literacy in African American communities.* Mahwah, NJ: Erlbaum.

Hammer, C. S., & Weiss, A. L. (1999). Guiding language development: How African American mothers and their infants structure play interactions. *Journal of Speech, Language, and Hearing Research, 42*(5), 1219-1233.

Harris, N. S., Courchesne, E., Townsend, J., Carper, R. A., & Lord, C. (1999). Neuro anatomic contributions to slowed orienting of attention in children with autism. *Cognitive Brain Research, 8,* 61-71.

Hart, B., & Risley, T. R. (1995). *Meaningful differences in the everyday experiences of young American children.* Baltimore: Paul H. Brookes.

Hofer, M. A. (1988). On the nature and function of prenatal behavior. In W. Smotherman & S. Robinson (Eds.), *Behavior of the fetus* (pp. 3-18). Caldwell, NJ: Telford.

Huttenlocher, J. (1998). Language input and language growth. *Preventive Medicine: An International Journal Devoted to Practice & Theory, 27*(2), 195-199.

Huttenlocher, J., Haight, W., Bryk, A., & Seltzer, M. (1991). Early vocabulary growth: Relation to language input and gender. *Developmental Psychology, 27*(2), 236-248.

Johnson, D. W., & Johnson, R. T. (1994). *Learning together and alone* (4th ed.). Boston: Allyn and Bacon.

Kail, B. (1990). *The development of memory in children* (3rd ed.). New York: W. H. Freeman.

Kiester, E. (2001). Accents are forever. *Smithsonian, 31*(10), 14-15.

Kim, S., Ugurbil, K., & Strick, P. (1994). Activation of a cerebellar output nucleus during cognitive processing. *Science, 265,* 949-951.

Klaus, J. G. (1995). Epidemiologic features of brain injury in children: Occurrence, children of risk, causes and manner of injury, severity and outcomes. In S. H. Broman & M. E. Michel (Eds.), *Traumatic head injury in children* (pp. 22-39). New York: Oxford.

Kuhl, P. K. (1994). Learning and representation in speech and language. *Current Opinion in Neurobiology, 4*(8), 812-822.

Kwon, Y., & Lawson, A. E. (2000). Linking brain growth with the development of scientific reasoning ability and conceptual change during adolescence. *Journal of Research in Science Teaching, 37*(1), 44-62.

LaHoste, G. J., Swanson, J. M., Wigal, S. B., Glabe, C., Wigal, T., King, N., & Kennedy, J. L. (1996). Dopamine D4 receptor gene polymorphism is associated with hyperactivity disorder. *Molecular Psychiatry, 1*(2), 121-124.

Lashley, K. (1950). *In search of the engram. Society for Experimental Biology #4: Mechanisms in animal behavior.* New York: Cambridge University Press.

Lezak, M. D. (1995). *Neuropsychological assessment* (3rd ed.). New York: Oxford.

Lichtman, J. W. (2001). Developmental neurobiology overview: Synapses, circuits, and plasticity. In D. B. Bailey, J. T. Bruer, F. J. Symons, & J. W. Lichtman (Eds.), *Critical thinking about critical periods* (pp. 27-42). Baltimore: Paul H. Brookes.

Lock, J. L. (1993). *The child's path to spoken language.* Cambridge, MA: Harvard University Press.

Locke, S., & Yakovlev, P. (1965). Transcallosal connections of the cingulum. *Transactions of the American Neurological Association, 90,* 176-178.

Lovaas, O., & Smith, T. (1988). Intensive behavioral treatment for younger autistic children. In B. B. Lahev & A. E. Kazdin (Eds.), *Advances in clinical psychology* (pp. 285-324). New York: Plenum Press.

Luria, A. R. (1973). *The working brain: An introduction to neuropsychology* (Trans., B. Haigh). New York: Basic Books.

MacLean, P. (1978). A mind of three minds: Educating the triune brain. In J. Chall & A. Mirsky (Eds.), *Education and the brain: 77th National Society for the Study of Education yearbook* (pp. 308-342). Chicago: Chicago University Press.

McIsaac, H., & Polick, J. (1992). Comparison of infant and adult P300 from auditory stimuli. *Journal of Experimental Child Psychology, 53,* 115-28.

Meyer, M. S. (2000). The ability-achievement discrepancy: Does it contribute to an understanding of learning disabilities? *Educational Psychology Review, 12*(3), 315-337.

Miller, G., Church, R., & Trexler, M. (2000). Teaching diverse learners using robotics. In A. Druin & J. Hendler (Eds.), *Robots for kids: Exploring new technologies for learning* (pp. 166-191). San Francisco: Morgan Kaufmann.

Mira, M., Tucker, B. F., & Tyler, J. S. (1992). *Traumatic brain injury in children and adolescents: A sourcebook for teachers and other school personnel.* Austin, TX: Pro-Ed.

Molfese, D. L., Molfese, V. J., & Espy, K. A. (1999). The predictive use of event-related potentials in language development and the treatment of language disorders. *Developmental Neuropsychology, 16*(3), 373-377.

Morrison, F. J., Alberts, D. M., & Griffith, E. M. (1997). Nature-nurture in the classroom: Entrance age, school readiness and learning in children. *Developmental Psychology, 33*(2), 254-262.

Mueller, R. A., Rothermel, R. D., Behen, M. E., Muzik, O., Mangner, T. J., & Chugani, H. T. (1998). Developmental changes of cortical and cerebellar motor control: A clinical positron emission tomography study with children and adults. *Journal of Child Neurology, 13*(11), 550-556.

National Institutes of Child Health and Human Development (NICHD). (1999). *NICHD study of early child care* [On-line, March 3, 1999].

National Institutes of Child Health and Human Development (NICHD). (2001, April). *Early child care and children's development prior to school entry. NICHD Early Child Care Research Network.* Paper presented at the Biennial Conference of the Society for Research in Child Development, Minneapolis, MN.

Nelson, C. A., & Bloom, F. E. (1997). Child development and neuroscience. *Child Development, 68*(5), 970-987.

Nelson, C. A., & Carver, L. (1998). The effects of stress and trauma on brain and memory: A view from developmental cognitive neuroscience. *Development and Psychopathology, 10*(4), 793-809.

Nelson, C. A., Monk, C. S., Lin, J., Carver, L. J., Thomas, K. M., & Truwit, C. L. (2000). Functional neuroanatomy of spatial working memory in children. *Developmental Psychology, 36*(1), 109-116.

Netting, J. (2001). Gray matters: Neurons get top billing but lesser-known brain cells also star. *Science News, 159,* 222-223.

Omaha World Herald (Associated Press report). (1999, May 16). *Bach-a-bye baby: Academy gives classical music CDs to babies,* 16-A.

Ornstein, R., & Thompson, R. F. (1984). *The amazing brain.* Boston: Houghton-Mifflin.

Panksepp, J. (1998). Attention deficit hyperactivity disorders, psychostimulants, and intolerance of childhood playfulness: A tragedy in the making? *Current Directions in Psychological Science, 7*(3), 91-98).

Park, N. W., & Ingles, J. L. (2000). Effectiveness of attention rehabilitation after an acquired brain injury: A meta-analysis. *Neuropsychology, 15*(2), 199-210.

Pellegrini, A., & Bjorklund, D. F. (1996). The place of recess in school: Issues in the role of recess in children's education and development (Introduction to theme issue, J. Johnson, Theme Coordinator.) *Journal of Research in Childhood Education, 11*(1), 5-13.

Pennington, B. (1995). Genetics of learning disabilities. *Journal of Child Neurology, 10 Suppl* 1(Jan), S69-77.

Perry, B. D. (1996). Incubated in terror: Neurodevelopmental factors in the "cycle of violence." In J. D. Osofsky (Ed.), *Children, youth and violence: Searching for solutions* (pp. 2-20). New York: Guilford.

Piaget, J. (1952). *The origins of intelligence in children.* New York: International Universities Press.

Piven, J. (1997). The biological basis of autism. *Current Opinion in Neurobiology, 7,* 708-712.

Piven, J., & O'Leary, D. (1997). Neuroimaging in autism. *Child and Adolescent Psychiatric Clinics of North America, 6*(2), 305-323.

Powers, W. J. (1990). Stroke. In A. L. Pearlman & R. C. Collins (Eds.), *Neurobiology of disease* (pp. 339-355). New York: Oxford University Press.

Puckett, M., Marshall, C. S., Davis, R. (1999). Examining the emergence of brain development research: The promises and the perils. *Childhood Education, 76,* 8-12.

Rakic, P. (1995). Corticogenesis in human and nonhuman primates. In M. S. Gazzaniga (Ed.), *The cognitive neurosciences* (pp. 127-145). Cambridge, MA: MIT.

Rakic, P., Bourgeois, J. P., & Goldman-Rakic, P. S. (1994). Synaptic development of the cerebral cortex: Implications for learning, memory, and mental illness. *Progress in Brain Research, 102,* 227-243.

Ramey, C. T., & Ramey, S. L. (1999). *Right from birth: Building your child's foundation for life.* New York: Goddard.

Rutter, M., Chadwick, O., Schaffer, D., & Brown, C. (1980). A prospective study of children with head injuries: I. Description and methods. *Psychological Medicine, 10,* 633-645.

Schopler, E. (1996). Implementation of TEACCH philosophy. In D. J. Cohen & F. R. Volkmar (Eds.), *The handbook of autism and pervasive developmental disorders* (pp. 767-795). New York: Plenum Press.

Shankle, W., Landing, B., Rafii, M., Schiano, A., Chen, J., & Hara, J. (1998). Evidence for a postnatal doubling of neuron number in the developing human cerebral cortex between 15 months and 6 years. *Journal of Theoretical Biology, 191*(2), 115-140.

Shaywitz, S. E., Shaywitz, B. A., Pugh, K. R., Fulbright, R. K., Constable, R. T., Memel, W. E., Shankweiler, D. P., Liberman, R. M., Skudlarski, P., Gletcher, J. M., Katz, L., Marchione, K. E., Lacadie, C., Gatenby, C., & Gore, J. C. (1998). *Proceedings of the National Academy of Sciences of the United States, 95*(5), 2636-2641.

Shonkoff, J. P., & Phillips, D. A. (Eds.). (2000). *From neurons to neighborhoods: The science of early childhood education.* Washington, DC: Institute of Medicine, National Academic Press.

Shore, R. (1997). *Rethinking the brain: New insights into early development.* New York: Families and Work Institute.

Slavin, R. E. (1995). *Cooperative learning: Theory, research, and practice* (2nd ed.). Boston: Allyn and Bacon.

Smolak, L., & Weintraub, M. (1983). Maternal speech: Strategy or response? *Journal of Child Language, 10*(2), 369-380.

Sylwester, R. (1995). *A celebration of neurons: An educator's guide to the human brain.* Alexandria, VA: Association for Supervision and Curriculum Development.

Tallal, P., Miller, S., Bedi, G., Byma, G., Wang, X., Nagarajan, S., Schreiner, C., Jenkins, W., & Merzenich, M. (1996). Language comprehension in language-learning impaired children improved with acoustically modified speech. *Science, 271,* 81-84.

Taylor, G. H., Drotar, D., Wade, S., Yeates, K., Stancin, T., & Klein, S. (1995). Recovery from traumatic brain injury in children: The importance of the family. In S. H. Broman & M. E. Michel (Eds.), *Traumatic head injury in children* (pp. 188-216). New York: Oxford.

Taylor, H. G., Klein, N., Minich, N. M., & Hack, M. (2000). Middle-school-age outcomes in children with very low birthweight. *Child Development, 71*(6), 1495-1511.

Thatcher, R. W. (1994). Cyclic cortical reorganization: Origins of human cognitive development. In G. Dawson & K. W. Fischer (Eds.), *Human behavior and the developing brain* (pp. 232-266). New York: Guilford Press.

Thompson, P. M., Giedd, J. N., Woods, R. P., MacDonald, D., Evans, A., & Toga, A. W. (2000). Growth patterns in the developing brain detected by using continuum mechanical tensor maps. *Nature, 404,* 190-193.

Thompson, R. A., & Nelson, C. A. (2001). Developmental science and the media: Early brain development. *American Psychologist, 56*(1), 5-15.

Tomasello, M., Mannie, S., & Kruger, A. C. (1986). Linguistic environment of 1- to 2-year-old twins. *Developmental Psychology, 22*(20), 169-176.

Topping, K., Holmes, E. A., & Brenner, W. (2000). The effectiveness of school-based programs for the promotion of social competence. In R. Bar-On & J. Parker (Eds.), *The handbook of emotional intelligence: Theory, development, assessment, and application at home, school, and in the workplace* (pp. 411-432). San Francisco: Jossey-Bass.

Travis, F. (1998). Cortical and cognitive development in 4th, 8th, and 12th grade students: The contribution of speed of processing and executive functioning to cognitive development. *Biological Psychology, 48*(1), 37-56.

Tremblay, G. C., & Peterson, L. (1999). Prevention of childhood injury: Clinical and public policy challenges. *Clinical Psychology Review, 19*(4), 415-434.

Warrick, P. D., & Naglieri, J. A. (1993). Gender differences in planning, attention, simultaneous, and successive (PASS) cognitive processes. *Journal of Educational Psychology, 85*(4), 693-701.

Weber-Fox, C., & Neville, H. J. (1996). Maturational constraints on functional specializations for language processing; ERP and behavioral evidence in bilingual speakers. *Journal of Cognitive Neuroscience, 8*(3), 231-256.

Wood, F. B., Flowers, D. L., & Buchsbaum, M. S. (1991). Investigation of abnormal left temporal functioning in dyslexia through rCBF, auditory evoked potential responses and positron emission tomography. *Reading and Writing Interdisciplinary Journal, 4*, 81-95.

Zeffiro, T., & Eden, G. (2000). The neural basis of developmental dyslexia. In L. Ganschow (Ed.), *Annals of dyslexia* (Vol. 50, pp. 3-30). Baltimore: International Dyslexia Association.

Glossary of Terms

Afferent nerves. Nerves that conduct impulses toward the central nervous system or its higher centers.

Amygdala. A large group of nuclei that are part of the subcortical gray matter in the temporal lobe.

Autonomic nervous system. The portion of the central nervous system that regulates involuntary actions.

Axon. The part of the neuron that transmits action potentials from the cell body to other neurons, muscles, or glands.

Basal ganglia. A group of structures deep in the cerebral hemispheres involved in inhibition of motor movements.

Brain stem. The section of the brain that includes the diencephalion (thalamus and hypothalamus), midbrain, and hindbrain.

Cerebellum. A structure in the hindbrain specialized for motor coordination; also plays a role in learning and memory.

Cerebrum. The rounded structure of the brain occupying most of the cranial cavity; divided into two hemispheres.

CNS. The central nervous system, including the brain and spinal cord.

Corpus callosum. The fiber system that connects the two hemispheres of the cerebrum.

Cortex. The outer layer of the brain with 4 to 6 layers of cells.

Cortical migration. A process of the prenatal period, in which neurons travel from lower brain areas to form the cortex.

Dendrites. The treelike structures of the neuron that receive information from the axons of other neurons.

Efferent nerves. Nerves that conduct impulses away from higher centers in the central nervous system toward muscles or glands.

Fissure. A deep cleft produced by folds of the cortex that extends to the ventricles.

Forebrain. The portion of the brain that includes the cerebral hemispheres, basal ganglia, thalamus, amygdala, hippocampus, and septum.

Frontal lobe. The portion of the cortex forward of the central sulcus.

Glia. The brain cells that provide support for the neurons and central nervous system.

Gyri. Convolutions of the cortex in the cerebral hemispheres.

Hemisphere lateralization. Specialization of functions in the two cerebral hemispheres.

Hindbrain. The region of the brain that contains the cerebellum, medulla, pons, and fourth ventricle.

Hippocampus. A primitive corticle structure in the anterior medial region of the temporal lobe, involved in memory, learning, and emotions.

Hypothalamus. A structure below the thalamus, involved in regulation of nearly all behavior (movement, feeding, sexual activity, sleeping, emotional expression, temperature, and endocrine production).

Limbic system. The neural systems that line the inside wall of the cortex, surrounding the corpus callosum and brain stem; primarily involved in learning, memory, and emotions.

Medulla. The portion of the hindbrain near the spinal cord; regulates reflexes and blood pressure.

Midbrain. The short segment between the forebrain and hindbrain.

Myelin. The lipid substance that forms an insulating sheath around certain nerve fibers.

Myelination. Formation of myelin on axons; myelination can be used as an index of brain maturation.

Neuron. The basic unit of the nervous system; its function is to transmit and store information (includes cell body, dendrites, and an axon).

Neurotransmitters. Chemicals released from synapses in response to action potentials; chemically transmit information from one neuron to another; examples of these are cortisol, serotonin, and dopamine.

Occipital lobes. The regions of the cortex lying in the back of the head.

Parietal lobes. The regions of the cortex lying beneath the parietal bone.

Phrenology. The discredited study of a relationship between the skull's surface and mental faculties.

Pineal body. A structure involved in circadian rhythms; initially thought by Descartes to be the location of the soul.

Pituitary gland. A structure at the base of the hypothalamus; involved in regulation of the endocrine system, which releases hormones.

Planum temporale. The cortical area behind the auditory cortex.

Pruning. The process by which synapses are eliminated.

Reticular activating system. The nerve cells and fibers in the brain stem, extending from the spinal cord to the thalamus.

Sulci. Small clefts produced by the folding of the cortex; not as deep as fissures.

Synapse. The point where nerve cells make contact; junction between an axonal terminal and a dendrite of another cell.

Synaptogenesis. The process by which synapses multiply.

Temporal lobes. The regions of the cortex lying laterally on the sides of the head.

Teratogens. Substances such as nicotine, alcohol, and cocaine that may negatively affect prenatal or later development.

Thalamus. The structure that relays visual, auditory, and sensory information to and from the cortex.

Ventricles. The cavities of the brain that contain cerebrospinal fluid.